CONTENTS

Published with assistance from the Mary Cady Tew Memorial Fund.

Designed by Nancy Ovedovitz and set in Caledonia type by Ro-Mark Typographic Co., Inc. Printed in the United States of America by Edwards Brothers, Inc., Ann Arbor, Michigan.

Library of Congress Cataloging in Publication Data

Simmel, Georg, 1858–1918.
    Georg Simmel: on women, sexuality, and love.
    Bibliography: p.
    Includes index.
    1. Women—Addresses, essays, lectures. 2. Feminism—Addresses, essays, lectures. 3. Culture—Addresses, essays, lectures. 4. Sex—Addresses, essays, lectures. 5. Love—Addresses, essays, lectures. I. Oakes, Guy. II. Title.
HQ1206.S54 1984   305.4   83-51292
ISBN 0-300-03195-5

10   9   8   7   6   5   4   3   2   1

GEORG SIMMEL: ON WOMEN, SEXUALITY, AND LOVE

Translated and with an
Introduction by Guy Oakes

Yale University Press
New Haven and London

GEORG SIMMEL: ON WOMEN, SEXUALITY, AND LOVE

between the Sexes" appeared in 1898.[2] Two years later, these ideas were incorporated into *The Philosophy of Money*, which also included a discussion of the monetary valuation of women, marriage, and prostitution.[3] A preliminary sketch of "Female Culture" appeared in 1902 (*Neue Deutsche Rundschau* 13: 504-15). This was followed by some remarks on the psychology of women in 1904, notes on the ideal of a philosophy of love in 1907, and a preliminary version of the essay "Flirtation" in 1909.[4] The year 1912 saw the publication of several brief articles on love and women in the works of Goethe,[5] material that was incorporated into Simmel's book on Goethe in the following year.

Much of the work on this book was done during my tenure as Max Weber Visiting Professor in the Institute for Sociology at Heidelberg University in the winter semester, 1982-83. I am grateful to the members of the Institute, and especially to Wolfgang Schluchter, for the congenial working conditions I enjoyed there. For advice on the translation, thanks are due to Thomas Burger, Charles Lewis, and Robert Canavan; for help with the final draft and the index, to Helene Glazer. This work was supported by a grant from Monmouth College (New Jersey) and a 1982 Summer Research Stipend from the National Endowment for the Humanities.

2. "Die Rolle des Geldes in den Beziehungen der Geschlechter. Fragment aus einer 'Philosophie des Geldes,'" published in the Viennese newspaper *Die Zeit*, Jan. 15, 22, and 29, 1898.

3. See Simmel 1978, chapter 5. This relationship between women, money, and prostitution was discussed as early as 1892 in Simmel's treatise on ethical theory. See *Einleitung in die Moralwissenschaft*, volume 1, pp. 195-212 (1964).

4. "Bruchstücke aus einer Psychologie der Frauen," *Der Tag*, Berlin, July 9, 1904; "Fragment aus einer Philosophie der Liebe," *Jugend*, Munich, 12, Dec. 1907, pp. 242-44; "Psychologie der Koketterie," *Der Tag*, Berlin, May 11-12, 1909.

5. "Goethe und die Frauen," *Petersburger Monatsblatt*, 1912, Nr. 463; "Goethe und die Frauen," *Ostsee-Zeitung*, Stettin, Sept. 28, 1912; "Goethe und die Frauen," *Potsdamer Tageszeitung*, Oct. 5, 1912; "Goethes Liebe," *Frankfurter Zeitung*, July 21, 1912.

ACKNOWLEDGMENTS

"Female Culture"is a translation of "Weibliche Kultur," first published in the *Archiv für Sozialwissenschaft und Sozialpolitik* (33 [1911]: 1–36) and included in the volume Simmel entitled *Philosophische Kultur: Gesammelte Essais* (Leipzig: Klinkhardt, 1911). A second edition of this book, which included some additional essays, appeared in 1919 (Leipzig: Kröner) and a third edition in 1923 (Potsdam: Gustav Kiepenheuer Verlag). Simmel also published "The Relative and the Absolute in the Problem of the Sexes" ("Das Relative und das Absolute im Geschlechterproblem") and "Flirtation" ("Die Koketterie") in this volume. The text of the third edition was used for the translations.

"On Love" is taken from the large body of material left unpublished at Simmel's death in September 1918. It first appeared as "Fragmente über die Liebe: Aus dem Nachlass Georg Simmels" in the journal *Logos* (10 [1921–22]: 1–54) and was included under the title "Über die Liebe (Fragment)" in the collection *Fragmente und Aufsätze aus dem Nachlass und Veröffentlichungen der letzten Jahre* (Munich: Drei-Masken-Verlag, 1923; reprinted by Georg Olms Verlagsbuchhandlung, Hildesheim, 1967). No previous English translations of these materials have been published.

Throughout his career, Simmel wrote regularly on issues concerning women, sexuality, and love. An essay "On the Psychology of Women" appeared in 1890, followed by brief newspaper pieces and popular journal articles on the women's movement in 1892, 1894, and 1896.[1] A newspaper piece on "The Role of Money in the Relations

---

1. "Zur Psychologie der Frauen," *Zeitschrift für Völkerpsychologie und Sprachwissenschaft* 20 (1890): 6–46; "Ein Jubiläum der Frauenbewegung," Sunday Supplement 48 of the *National-Zeitung* of Nov. 27, 1892; "Der Militarismus und die Stellung der Frauen," Sunday Supplements 42 and 43 of the *Vossische Zeitung* of Oct. 28, 1894; "Der Frauenkongress und die Sozialdemokratie," *Die Zukunft* 17 (1896): 80–84.

TRANSLATOR'S INTRODUCTION

THE PROBLEM OF WOMEN
IN SIMMEL'S THEORY OF CULTURE

SIMMEL'S PROBLEMATIC AND THE
PHENOMENON OF OBJECTIFICATION

Objectivity is the specifically human quality: instead of an interest in the subject (regardless of whether this is meant in a more vulgar or a more elevated sense), an interest in the things themselves. We want to know what the properties of things are simply in order that we may be cognizant of this objective fact. We act in order to realize a certain state of affairs that is of absolutely no personal concern to us. We serve God without thinking of a reward, purely as a consequence of the logic of our relationship to the absolute. We attempt to give our own lives a value, simply in order that this value may have an objective status, without any real or ideal reflexive relationship to the self. This is the practical embodiment of the purely spiritual fact that the human being can become its own object.[1]

In an observation that is typically Simmelian—ambivalent and cryptic, yet also suggestive and provocative—Simmel once described the definitive problem of his work as "the objectification of the subject, or rather the desubjectification of the individual" (Simmel 1967, p. 4). The essays in this volume may be taken as sketches of several closely related perspectives from which this problem is explored. In Simmel's view, the discovery of objectivity—the independence of things from the conditions of their subjective or psychological genesis—was the greatest achievement in the cultural history of the West. Plato discovered the objectivity of the mind, Roman law the objectivity of justice, and Roman Catholicism the objectivity of religion (Simmel 1967, pp. 42–43). It was left to a complex and remarkably heterogeneous German tradition in philosophy and the sociocultural sciences—from Herder and Kant through Hegel and Schleiermacher to Marx and Dilthey, and perhaps ultimately con-

1. From an undated entry in Simmel's posthumously published journals. See Simmel 1967, p. 22.

3

summated in the work of Max Weber—to discover the sense in which culture itself is a condition for objectivity.

In all of his major writings from the publication of *The Philosophy of Money* in 1900 to his death in 1918, there is a set of problems to which Simmel repeatedly returned. It is clear that they formed the principal interest in the research he undertook during this period. It is also evident that they were quite intimately related in his thought, even though he never made the precise relationship explicit. Although Simmel articulated these problems in different ways, they were invariably concerned with the complexities and variations of the relationship between human life and the forms in which it is structured. There seem to be two basic aspects of this relationship. On the one hand, forms are necessary conditions for the expression and the realization of the energies and interests of life. On the other hand, these same forms become increasingly detached and remote from life. When this happens, a conflict develops between the process of life and the configurations in which it is expressed. Ultimately, this conflict threatens to nullify the relationship between life and form, and thus to destroy the conditions under which the process of life can be realized in autonomous structures.

In *The Philosophy of Money*, for example, Simmel argues that the institutions in which the money economy is universalized are essential to the development of individual freedom. Yet these same institutions also represent a world of forms in which the freedom of the individual is progressively restricted. In the final analysis, the forces that originally functioned as conditions for the possibility of freedom threaten to destroy it. In his book on Kant, Simmel ascribes the same ambivalent consequences to theoretical processes that are closely linked with the universalization of the money economy: the mathematization and mechanization of the world, the reduction of qualities to quantities, and the intellectualization of the world achieved in the attempt to explain all phenomena by reference to the operation of a single set of laws. In many of the seminal essays of this period, Simmel documents the conflict between life and form in a variety of phenomena. The tension between the theoretical aims of the individual scientist and the division of scientific labor; the discrepancy between the authentic religious experience and the ecclesiastical institutions to which this experience must accommodate itself; the struggle between the integrity of artistic expression and the aesthetic forms in which the artist is obliged to cast his work: These are only a few of the areas in which Simmel investigates the opposition between the process of life and the forms in which it is defined. In some of his most brilliantly suggestive studies, Simmel establishes how this conflict achieves a concrete and dramatic expression within the life of a single person. For example, in his work on individual philosophers and artists, Simmel examines the varying relations between subjectivity and objectivity by focusing upon the manner in which human experience creates a novel form of individuality that either resolves this conflict in a new synthesis or suspends it in a new field of force. He is especially intrigued by the creative individual, the virtuoso or genius of cultural innovation who attempts to interpret and transform the conflict between life and form in a novel fashion, or even a revolutionary direction. Kant and Goethe, Schopenhauer and Nietzsche, Rembrandt and Michelangelo, Stefan George and August Rodin are among Simmel's favorite exemplars of these cultural innovators and revolutionaries.[2]

In the first two essays in this volume, Simmel explores the conditions for the objectification of the female experience, the problematical character of this process, and its clash with the predominantly male culture in which the woman finds herself. In the final analysis, the woman becomes estranged from a world of cultural modalities and artifacts that cannot be reconciled with her mode of being, a result that leads Simmel to consider the possibility of a distinctively female culture. In the essay on flirtation, the behavior of the coquette is analyzed as an expression of the simultaneous surrender and withdrawal of the self, an experience objectified in a form of life that intersects with femininity, sexuality, and play. As an interpretive category, however, Simmel extends flirtation beyond the behavior of the coquette in the narrow sense to consider two especially

---

2. See, for example, *Kant und Goethe* (1906), *Schopenhauer und Nietzsche* (1923b), *Goethe* (1913), and *Rembrandt* (1919). See also Simmel's essays on Michelangelo (1923a, pp. 147–84), Stefan George (1922b, pp. 22–45), and Rodin (1923a, pp. 185–203). His contemporary and sometime discussion partner, the theologian and historian Ernst Troeltsch, claims that it was only a lack of musicological expertise that prevented Simmel from including Beethoven in this series of metaphysical biographies. See Troeltsch 1922, pp. 586–87.

interesting cases. In the relationship between flirtation and intellectuality, the intellectual performance is expressed as a form of apparently indecisive erotic play, enticing the audience of the performance, but to an end that it cannot fathom. And in the relationship between flirtation and politics, flirtation functions as power, the expression of the coquette's freedom and her—or his—ability to dominate the partner who serves as the object of erotic attraction. In the final essay, Simmel considers love as a phenomenon generated by life in the nascent or rudimentary proto-form of sexual attraction. However, when the erotic mode of existence develops its own distinctive configurations and begins to function according to its own principles, one of the axial inversions or revolutions characteristic of Simmel's thought takes place. Although love is an instrument that serves the procreative needs of life, it now becomes an end in itself. Life is employed as an instrument to realize the existentially autonomous purposes of love. As a result, the erotic existence becomes detached from life and irreconcilable with its interests, an antagonism which is perhaps most clearly expressed in the conflict between the passions of eroticism and the forms of marriage.

CULTURE AND OBJECTIFICATION

Thus the essays in this volume focus upon a collection of closely related phenomena. They all pose the problem of how certain modes of existence which Simmel regards as fundamental to human life—being male or female, the experience of sexuality, the different ways in which sexuality defines the being of men and women and the relations between them, the experience of loving and being an object of love, the variety of erotic experiences and their bearing upon the male and the female existence—are translated into structures that transform life itself. These phenomena and the questions they raise for Simmel are situated in the domain he calls culture: the process in which life first reproduces itself as "more life" and then transcends itself by generating forms that qualify as "more-than-life." Simmel represents culture as a two-dimensional process. On the one hand, the energies and interests of life are defined and molded by the forms of "objective culture," the world of cultural forms and their artifacts that have become independent of individual human existence. Objective culture is the domain of objects that function as instruments for the cultivation of the person, or as conditions under which he can become a cultural being. On the other hand, these cultural forms and their artifacts are incorporated into the "subjective culture" of the individual, the state of the personality which is the ultimate result of the process of cultivation and which represents a synthesis of the world of cultural forms. Subjective culture is the personal culture of the individual, or the life of the individual as a cultural being.[3]

The objection that Simmel's thought assumes a static relationship between life and form has repeatedly been raised by his neo-Marxist critics, especially those influenced by Lukács.[4] In the preface to the 1967 edition of *History and Class Consciousness*, Lukács criticizes Simmel's work on the grounds that it illegitimately "ontologizes" the cultural forms and artifacts of the Wilhelmian era, in effect interpreting them as "the timeless model of human relations in general" (Lukács 1971, pp. xxiii–xxiv). This allegedly commits Simmel to a species of depoliticized sociological aestheticism. Simmelian social science is a purely contemplative theoretical enterprise, withdrawn from all normative commitments.[5] Although it may indeed be true that Simmel ontologized Wilhelmian culture by taking it as the paradigm of sociocultural reality as such, it is not clear why this should qualify as a valid criticism of his theory of culture. The important issue is whether that theory is sound, a question to which Lukács's objection seems to be irrelevant. In fact, it could be said that every sociocultural theory employs certain paradigms of sociocultural reality on the basis of which other aspects of society and culture are interpreted and explained. In this sense, Marx ontologized the

---

3. The distinction between subjective and objective culture is analyzed in the translator's introduction to Simmel 1980. For Simmel's somewhat nebulous account of what is at stake here, see the remarks on the concept of the objective spirit as a condition for the possibility of culture in his book *Hauptprobleme der Philosophie*, 1910, p. 72.

4. See Lieber and Furth 1958; Adorno 1965; and Lieber 1974.

5. There is a more detailed version of the same objections in the fourth chapter of Lukács's *The Destruction of Reason* (1981). The suggestion that Simmel's sociology "aestheticizes" reality also seems to be the main thesis of David Frisby's recent reassessment of his work (1981).

process of commodity production in the British textile industry of the mid-nineteenth century in *Capital*; Weber ontologized the conduct of the early Puritan entrepreneur in *The Protestant Ethic and the Spirit of Capitalism*; Burkhardt ontologized the experience of the fifteenth-century northern Italian urban tyrant in *The Civilization of the Renaissance in Italy*; and Freud ontologized his own experience in *The Interpretation of Dreams*. This sort of reasoning may be motivated by all sorts of considerations. Although these motives may prove to be of immense interest to a history or a psychology of the theoretician or to a sociology of science, they are ultimately irrelevant to the question of the validity of the theory in which the assumption is made. That question can be resolved only by determining whether the assumption is fruitful for the interpretation of the meaning of sociocultural artifacts or the explanation of their genesis and consequences.

In addition, it can be said that this neo-Marxist critique of Simmel's work ignores his view of the interaction between life and form. This is why Lieber, for example, mistakenly ascribes to Simmel an absolute dichotomy between historical forms and historical phenomena. It is also why he interprets Simmel's sociology as an ahistorical social ontology (Lieber 1974, p. 78). As regards this interpretation of Simmel's theory of forms, three points should be noted. First, Simmel himself must share the responsibility for this distortion of his views. Especially in his book *Soziologie* (1908), Simmel's language sometimes suggests that he is committed to a static and absolute dichotomy of form and life. Consider, for example, his suggestion that sociology may be conceived as a kind of geometry of social forms (Wolff 1959, p. 320), a metaphor that obviously encourages this interpretation. Second, Simmel's conception of form cannot be understood independent of his epistemological and metaphysical writings that are devoted to the project of elucidating the relationship between life and form.[6] It follows that an interpretation confined to an analysis of *Soziologie*—and this is the strategy employed by Lieber and Furth— can be expected to result in considerable distortion. Finally, the meaning of the Simmelian concept of form does not remain constant

---

6. See especially *The Problems of the Philosophy of History*, chapter 1 (1977), *Goethe* (1913), *Kant* (1921), and *Lebensanschauung* (1922a).

throughout his work. The changes become especially important in the period of his thought that begins with the publication of his book on Goethe in 1913. In fact, the relationship between life and form appears more clearly in the works Simmel published after *Soziologie*. This holds true especially for the essays he wrote on the nature of modern culture, the most important of which appeared during World War I. Concentration on an early work—Lieber and Furth, for example, are mainly concerned with an analysis of the first chapter of *Soziologie*, which originally appeared as a journal article in 1894—ignores the development of Simmel's position.

Simmel's essays on the processes, artifacts, and forms of culture typically focus on four issues: the manner in which life creates cultural forms; the modes in which these forms become "objectified," Simmel's term for the transformations of the structures of culture that result in their remoteness from life and their relative inaccessibility to individuals; the distinctive qualities of objectified forms and their expression in the lives and social relations of individuals; and, finally, the problematical consequences generated by the process of objectification. Simmel's conception of culture as the objectification of human experience is an essential premise of the positions he takes in the subsequent essays. Culture is the process in which the modes of existence explored here are expressed and realized. This is why Simmel's analyses of femininity, sexuality, flirtation, and erotics can be traced and his intentions grasped only by clarifying his informal and fragmentary remarks on the nature of culture and exposing its definitive features. This is the purpose of the following two sections, which consider the two essential aspects of culture as the objectification of life: the reification and the instrumentalization of cultural forms.

OBJECTIFICATION AS REIFICATION

On the one hand, Simmel's theory of culture presupposes that cultural forms are conditions for the constitution of the individual personality and the formation of its identity. This is why the subjective culture of the individual depends upon the objective culture of the artifacts he produces. On the other hand, there are various respects in which objective culture can become detached from the life of the individual. This occurs whenever cultural artifacts can be only incompletely incorporated into his subjective culture. Because the products of objective culture exhibit a tendency to evolve into autonomous and self-contained "kingdoms" or "empires" (Simmel 1957, p. 94), the world of cultural artifacts becomes more complex, refined, systematic, and complete. However, the definitive process of culture—the synthesis of cultural forms in the life of the individual—does not proceed at the same rate. As a result, objective culture becomes increasingly self-contained and self-perpetuating, even though it can never reach the ideal limit of unconditional emancipation from subjective culture. Put another way, the development of culture follows a curve in which the progressive autonomy of objective culture approaches a limit that is never actually attained. This is because the possibility of objective culture depends upon the activity of persons who create artifacts that express the energies of their lives. In Simmel's language, culture is possible only if human life creates entities that qualify as more-than-life. But this exercise of the creative forces of life would be blocked if the structures of culture were completely independent of the persons whose activity is responsible for their production. Thus the complete emancipation of objective culture from its subjective genesis is impossible. It would mean that the subjective conditions on which objective culture depends are no longer satisfied.

What is responsible for this discrepancy between the development of objective culture and the more restricted formation of subjective culture? Although there are no limits in principle upon the expansion of objective culture, the development of subjective culture is determined by the capacity of the individual to incorporate the artifacts of objective culture into his own life. As the culture of things becomes more extensive, complex, and sophisticated, individuals are no longer able to consolidate this state of objective culture into a correspondingly advanced state of subjective culture. This development may be called the reification of cultural forms.

As an illustration of the process of reification that Simmel mentions but does not examine in any detail, consider the development of the sciences. The universal natural philosopher of the late seventeenth century disappears by the time of the French Revolution. Because of the relative harmony between the development of the objective culture of science and the possibilities of its subjective culture, scientists of the generation of Newton, Hooke, and Huygens could be equally comfortable in dealing with the problems of optics, mechanics, and astronomy. Because of the modest levels of scientific specialization, there is a sense in which it was possible for the individual scientist to incorporate the entire corpus of natural philosophy into his subjective scientific culture, an aspect of early modern science profusely illustrated in the correspondence of Henry Oldenburg, the secretary of the early Royal Society of London, who carried on a prodigious exchange of letters with both producers and consumers of scientific culture in Britain and on the Continent (Oldenburg 1965–69). The science of the early Royal Society, therefore, was the science of the gifted amateur and the virtuoso, the liberal scientific culture of the "gentleman free and unconfined." By the period of Benjamin Franklin and Joseph Priestley, this relationship between the subjective and objective culture of science was no longer possible. Although Enlightenment scientists were hardly specialists or careerists in the modern sense—this is notoriously true of Franklin, and Priestley was a Puritan divine who also wrote extensively on social and political issues—their scientific work was much more specialized than the research of the early members of the Royal Society. By the generation of Lavoisier and Laplace, the more intensive specialization that became the hallmark of nineteenth-century science appears.

As a science develops, it poses new problems that have no essential relationship to the interests that originally generated science as a cultural form. Novel scientific problems are produced by the immanent evolution of the science itself, a development that becomes detached from the research interests and the capacities of the individual scientist. The result is the disengagement of objective scientific culture both from the practical interests of everyday life and from the personal scientific culture of the individual scientist. As the problems posed by the growth of every science multiply and become more recondite, the inevitability of a more intensive specialization follows. The modern scientific careerist is a product of this process. The modern scientist is not a natural philosopher but rather a specialist within some clearly defined area of a specific subdiscipline. It is not possible for him to incorporate the entire domain of scientific problems into his own subjective scientific culture. It is not even possible for him to master all the problems of his own field. As specialized periodicals proliferate and reproduce themselves by creating generation upon generation of even more specialized journals, the individual scientist finds that the bulk of objective scientific culture has become impenetrable to him. His estrangement from the objective culture of science is expressed in the tension between the attempt to master the corpus of scientific knowledge—and above all to remain abreast of the most recent advances—and the attempt to maintain the integrity of his own scientific personality. On the one hand, there is no sense in which the scientist can incorporate the total universe of scientific discourse into his own personal research program. On the other hand, he cannot cheerfully dismiss the objective culture of science as unimportant or inconsequential. This is because it is a possible object of his own scientific culture. Each scientific artifact—every experiment, journal article, and discovery—is a possible source of enrichment of his scientific life and the advancement of his career. The result, Simmel notes, is a mood of oppression and a feeling of pessimism: The identity of the scientific personality is threatened by the reified world of scientific culture that the scientist can neither master nor escape.

In sum, the reification of cultural forms may be conceived both as a process and as a state of cultural development for which the following four conditions are essential. First, the existential content of some sphere of life—whether it be scientific, political, moral, religious, aesthetic, or erotic—is expressed in the artifacts of a cultural form. Second, this form becomes a relatively independent entity, self-contained, self-perpetuating, and developing according to its own immanent principles. As a result, it also becomes increasingly remote from the energies and interests that were originally invested in it. Finally, the development of this form outstrips the ability of the individual to master or control it. In consequence, he cannot incorporate its artifacts within the synthesis of his own personal culture.

When these conditions are satisfied, it can be said that reification has taken place within the domain of the cultural form in question. This process is more or less advanced depending upon the limits within which these conditions are satisfied. It can also be said that the cultural form is in a corresponding state of reification that is more or less advanced, again depending upon the extent to which these conditions are satisfied. Finally, it can be said that a culture is more or less reified, depending upon how many of its forms are implicated in this process. In the ensuing essays, Simmel will argue that there is a sense in which culture has become reified in a distinctively male direction. In other words, there is a sense in which reification also qualifies as masculinization. This circumstance generates special conflicts that define the predicament of women in relation to objective culture.

OBJECTIFICATION AS INSTRUMENTALIZATION

As a preliminary to the discussion of Simmel's account of instrumentalization, it may be useful to indicate some of the subtleties it involves. In examining the status of values in Simmel's theory of culture, two possibilities can be identified. On the one hand, there are certain actions and artifacts that express the synthesis of the forms of objective culture that is achieved by the individual human personality. They may be called authentic cultural values or, more conveniently, authentic values. On the other hand, there are actions and artifacts that do not qualify as authentic values but are rather conditions for their realization. A certain action, for example, might function as a necessary condition for the realization of a certain cultural value in spite of the fact that no authentic value can be ascribed to the action itself. Actions and artifacts that have this property may be called instrumental cultural values, or instrumental values.

Given this distinction, the instrumentalization of culture can be described in the following way. Consider the ensemble of instrumental and authentic values that defines every cultural form. Simmel calls such a configuration of values a teleological sequence. In some of these sequences, the intermediate, instrumental link is multiplied until the end of the sequence—which is responsible for the cultural value that can be ascribed to the sequence as a whole—can no longer be discerned. Because instrumental values appear to preempt or replace authentic values, there seems to be a sense in which means are transposed into ends. This process can be called axiological dislocation. In other teleological sequences, authentic values can actually be identified. However, they are not recognized as such but are rather conceived as if they were instrumental values. In this case, ends seem to be derogated to the level of means since authentic values are degraded to instrumental values. This process can be called axiological trivialization. Culture is axiologically dislocated in the sense that the status of authentic values is ascribed to instrumental values. It is axiologically trivialized in the sense that authentic values are represented as if they were nothing more than instrumental values with a purely utilitarian function. Axiological dislocation and axiological trivialization are the definitive processes of the instrumentalization of culture.[7]

According to Simmel, the instrumentalization of culture is responsible for the belief that life has become meaningless. This perception of the pointlessness or absurdity of life is the source of the qualities of personal life that typify advanced cultures: banality, decadence, narcissism, aestheticism, solipsism, skepticism, relativism, and nihilism. In the Occidental culture of late Classical Antiquity, the major contribution of Christianity was to resolve the problem of the meaning of life created by the increasing instrumentalization of culture (Simmel 1906, pp. 1–2; 1923b, pp. 1–3). This was achieved by situating the unconditional purpose and the ultimate meaning of life in the salvation of the soul and the Kingdom of God, which occupied the status of authentic values, transcending all the individual, fragmentary, and intrinsically meaningless contents of culture. Although Simmel notes that the capacity of Christianity to create authentic values seems to have waned, the axiological interest that it originally satisfied remains one of the vital conditions of a human existence. The need to ascribe an authentic value to the process of culture has not diminished to the same extent that the Christian response to this need has lost its power to produce conviction. On the contrary, precisely because this need was fulfilled by Christianity for so many

---

7. In light of the foregoing analysis, it should be clear that Simmel's conception of the instrumentalization of culture is closely related to the Marxian ideas of commodity fetishism and false consciousness. Given Simmel's position, false consciousness is the mentality that typifies an instrumentalized culture. Commodity fetishism is simply one instance of the general process of axiological dislocation in which instrumental values seem to acquire the status of authentic values.

centuries, it became deeply rooted in the mentality of advanced Occidental culture. In consequence, an ardent, profound, and yet apparently unsatisfiable passion for authentic values remains the dubious cultural precipitate of Christianity. It endures in spite of the fact that the authority of the cultural forms that originally met this need has very largely lapsed. In place of its former power to generate authentic values, Christianity has deposited the quest for a definitive purpose of life, an empty search for ends that have become unattainable.

This relationship between instrumentalization and the problem of an ultimate purpose or meaning of life is an important theme in *The Philosophy of Money*. As a result of instrumentalization, no member of the teleological sequence seems to be identifiable as an authentic value. This creates the disposition to impute such value to the sequence as a whole. As culture becomes axiologically trivialized, as ends are reduced to means and authentic values are degraded to the status of instrumental values, the need arises to ascribe some authentic value to the total process of culture. The relationship between instrumentalization and the problem of the meaning of life rests on a crucial assumption in Simmel's philosophical anthropology: Human beings cannot act without ascribing authentic values to their conduct. If such an axiological basis is essential to human action, and if it becomes increasingly difficult to locate any authentic value in the individual components of the teleological sequence, then this assumption accounts for the disposition to ascribe authentic value to the sequence as a whole.

It follows that there is a direct relationship between the process of instrumentalization and the transcendence of the values that are regarded as ultimate (Simmel 1978, p. 361). As the instrumentalization of culture advances, any putatively authentic value must be increasingly remote from the process of culture itself. This is because an immanent cultural value would be situated within the teleological sequence, in which case it would also be implicated in the process of instrumentalization and reduced to the status of a purely instrumental value. At this point, there is a temptation to formulate what might be called Simmel's Law of Modernity: The transcendence of authentic values is a function of the complexity of culture. Simple cultures characterized by a modest degree of instrumentalization will generate an immanent axiology.[8] Pantheistic religions in which god is identified with nature or is said to inhabit nature provide examples of such an axiology. Complex cultures characterized by a quantitatively extensive and qualitatively intensive degree of instrumentalization will generate a transcendent axiology. Monotheistic religions in which there is an absolute distinction between god and the world are examples of such a transcendent axiology. If this postulate identifies Simmel's view of the relationship between modernity and axiological transcendence, it follows that there can be no immanent values in modern culture.[9]

The instrumentalization of culture generates a chaotic multiplicity of cultural forms, Simmel's version of Max Weber's conception of the polytheism of values that is characteristic of modernity. Because an authentic value cannot be ascribed to any of these forms, it seems that no cultural value is preferable to any other. The belief that there are no qualitative differences between cultural values results in a relativism that leads to nihilism: the suspicion that if all cultural values have the same purely instrumental status, then there are no authentic cultural values. Thus the apparent paradox generated by the instrumentalization of culture may be formulated as follows: Although the process of culture creates the need to ascribe an ultimate purpose to life, it also destroys the conditions under which this need can be satisfied. It does not destroy the need itself, however,

8. In Simmel's work, the distinction between a higher and a lower culture or between a complex and a simple culture is based on two criteria: the internal differentiation or complexity of any given teleological sequence, and the number of different teleological sequences. Both the length of a given sequence and the number of different sequences are functions of the reification and instrumentalization of culture. Thus cultural complexity is defined by reference to the two constitutive processes of objectification. Modernity is an advanced state of these processes. In Simmel's theory of culture, therefore, the polar antithesis of the modern is neither the archaic nor the traditional but rather the undifferentiated.

9. Money, which is situated in the teleological sequences of culture but nevertheless seems to become an authentic value in a modern culture, is only an apparent exception to this "law." In Simmel's view, money is not really an authentic cultural value. It only seems to occupy this status in the consciousness of a reified and instrumentalized culture. Simmel's position on this issue, therefore, approximates the view of "the power of money in bourgeois society" that Marx takes in the Paris manuscripts of 1844.

the passion for authentic values and the longing for an ultimate purpose.[10] The role of money in modern culture is the Simmelian paradigm of the axiological trivialization of authentic values and the axiological dislocation of instrumental values. The cultural value of money is exhausted by two purely instrumental functions. First, it serves as a principle for standardizing values so that they can all be compared on the same scale. This function of money is a consequence of the fact that its value is completely determined by the relationship that obtains among other values. Because it expresses this relationship in a uniform and general fashion, money is the basis for measuring all other values. For this reason, it can also facilitate their exchange and serve as a medium of exchange. This is its second function. Moreover, money has only one quality: its quantity. Because no qualitatively distinctive properties can be ascribed to money, it is the absolutely interchangeable cultural artifact: Any given parcel of money can be replaced by any other parcel of the same quantity without any qualitative distinction or any loss of its distinctive properties. This is, of course, a consequence of the fact that money merely expresses a relationship between cultural values which can remain constant in spite of changes in the properties of the artifacts to which these values are ascribed.

According to Simmel, the importance of these two functions of money is a consequence of the number of qualitatively different artifacts produced by objective culture and the variability of the relations between them. In a culture in which the number of different artifacts is trifling and the relations between them remain relatively stable, the cultural value of money will be quite modest. As the number of different artifacts multiplies and the variability of their relations increases, the cultural value of money becomes more significant. Modernity generates a constantly increasing number of cultural artifacts, and the instability of its forms ensures that the relations between these artifacts will remain in flux. Thus in a modern culture,

---

10. This is an important instance of the doctrine of the tragedy of culture that Simmel sketches in "The Relative and the Absolute in the Problem of the Sexes" and "On Love." The Simmelian concept of the tragedy of culture is analyzed in the translator's introduction to Simmel 1980.

where qualitatively different values proliferate and vary, money as the pure or absolute means has a tendency to acquire the status of a pure or absolute value. This is why the modern preeminence of the cultural value of money is a paradigm case of instrumentalization. The fact that money has acquired the apparent status of an authentic cultural value is a result of the development of culture itself, which makes this otherwise irrational dislocation of value comprehensible. If every cultural value becomes a commodity with a determinate monetary value, and if every commodity is in principle accessible to every potential consumer, then the satisfaction of most human desires will depend exclusively upon whether the potential consumer of cultural values has enough money. From the perspective of the consciousness of modern culture, therefore, want or deficiency does not primarily signify an insufficiency of cultural artifacts but rather a lack of money. As a result, money, which was nothing more than an instrument for the standardization and exchange of values, becomes the paradigmatic value: the universal axiological solvent, the value by reference to which the worth of every other cultural artifact is defined. In Simmel's analysis, the axiological dislocation of money is intimately related to the collapse of authentic cultural values. Although traditional values no longer occupy this status, the disposition to ascribe some authentic value to the fragmentary and purely instrumental values of culture remains. Because modern culture seems to have destroyed, displaced, or concealed authentic values, an absolute axiological status is ascribed to the most perfect instrumental value: namely, money.[11]

11. This is one of the major themes of Thomas Mann's early novel *Buddenbrooks*. "Grünlich is bankrupt?"—thus the incredulous question of the bewildered merchant princess Tony Buddenbrooks upon learning that the commercial adventures of her deceitful husband have collapsed. "In that moment all that was involved in the word 'bankrupt' rose clearly before her: all the vague and fearful hints which she had heard as a child. 'Bankrupt'—that was more shameful than death, that was catastrophe, ruin, shame, disgrace, misery, despair" (Mann 1961, pp. 167–68). Bankruptcy, or total financial deprivation, is experienced as the total loss of value, the axiological ground zero, a relationship which of course presupposes that money occupies the status of the paradigmatic cultural value. On money and the instrumentalization of culture, see Simmel 1978, pp. 230–32, 236–38, 360–65, 481–84. Simmel also argues that the role of money in the process of instrumentalization is intimately related to the intellectualization of modern culture. See 1978, pp. 150–52, 172, 277–80, 311, 314–15, 431–36, 440–46, 476–79.

OBJECTIFICATION AND THE DIVISION OF LABOR

In sum, the objectification of culture includes two processes. On the one hand, the instruments of culture undergo a hypertrophy of growth and transcend their original functions and limits. As a result, many of these instruments apparently acquire the status and dignity of ultimate values and final purposes at the same time that authentic cultural values are degraded to the level of mere techniques. This is the process of instrumentalization. On the other hand, the structures of culture develop in a quasi-autonomous fashion and evolve according to their own immanent norms. When objectified forms become detached from the needs and interests of life, the tempo of their development can no longer be matched by the progress of subjective culture. As the sphere of objective culture constantly expands, an increasing number of cultural artifacts become inaccessible to the subjective culture of the individual. This is the process of reification.[12]

In Simmel's view, there is an intimate relationship between the process of objectification and the division of social and cultural labor. On the one hand, the division of labor is the principal motive force responsible for the divergence between subjective and objective culture that leads to objectification. On the other hand, the division of labor is also a consequence of the increasing distance between subjective and objective culture, and thus a product of objectification. However, the division of labor augments this distance as well, which in turn expands and intensifies the division of labor. Thus a dynamic and functional relationship seems to obtain between objectification and the division of labor. A given stage in the objectification of culture is possible only as a consequence of a corresponding level of the division of labor. This stage of objectifica-

---

12. Objectification as a pathological state of modern culture is one of the major themes of Hermann Broch's trilogy *The Sleepwalkers* (1947). See especially part 3, "The Realist." According to Broch, the immanent and relentless development of the military, commerce, art, and politics exhibits "that uncanny, I might almost say that metaphysical, lack of consideration for consequences, that ruthless logic directed on the object and on the object alone" (p. 446). As a result of the increasing sophistication and self-perpetuating evolution of incommensurable cultural spheres, the individual becomes "helplessly caught in the mechanism of the autonomous value systems." In the long run, he is "eaten up by the radical logic of the value into whose jaws he has fallen" (p. 448).

tion then generates a new level of the division of labor, which leads to a new stage of objectification.

Suppose that O stands for some stage of the objectification of culture and D designates some level of the division of labor. If the subscript $_t$ designates time, then: $O_t \rightarrow D_{t+1} \rightarrow O'_{t+2} \rightarrow D'_{t+3}$ etc. At $t+2$, the distance between subjective and objective culture is greater than at t. Thus the culture of O' is more objectified than the culture of O. And at $t+3$, the division of labor is more complex than at $t+1$. Thus the culture of D' is more specialized and highly differentiated than the culture of D.[13]

In the sixth chapter of *The Philosophy of Money*, Simmel examines the relationship between objectification and the division of labor by considering the conditions for the production and consumption of cultural artifacts in an advanced culture.[14] When cultural forms begin to develop according to their own immanent norms, the production of cultural artifacts becomes increasingly specialized. Ultimately, therefore, the division of labor seems to be a consequence of the increasing remoteness of objective culture from

13. In Frisby's discussion of this relationship, the division of labor is identified as the cause of objectification. (See Frisby 1981, pp. 123–24.) However, the reciprocal relationship between these two processes is not considered. Frisby discusses the consequences of the division of labor in chapter 4. The process of objectification and its consequences are described in chapters 4 and 5.

14. This discussion reproduces the major theses of Marx's theory of the social relations characteristic of the capitalist mode of production. Simmel generalizes Marx's account in two important respects. First, Marx's analysis of the commodity fetishism and alienation produced by the capitalist labor process is extended to the production of all cultural artifacts. This is an aspect of the relationship between Marx's interpretation of capitalism and Simmel's interpretation of modernity: Some of the definitive theses of Marx's account of capitalist culture are generalized to produce a theory of modern culture. Second, in Marx's discussion of alienation and commodity fetishism, he limits himself to an inquiry into the conditions for the production of commodities. Simmel extends this inquiry in order to consider the conditions for their consumption. This is one of the differences between the theoretical interests that motivate Marx's investigation of capitalism and Simmel's investigation of modernity. Because of Marx's interest in explaining the genesis and development of the capitalist process of production and discovering its "laws of motion," he concentrates on the social relations of production. Because of Simmel's interest in the conditions under which objective culture can be incorporated into subjective culture, he concentrates on the social relations of consumption.

the personal existence of individuals. Simmel notes that the specialization of the process of production perfects the product at the expense of the producer. As objective culture is enriched, subjective culture is impoverished. Specialized production requires specialized producers. However, the product does not express the character of the producer. On the contrary, its cultural value is a consequence of its relationship to other equally specialized products. As a result of the division of labor, therefore, the producer is estranged from the process of production, which becomes progressively objectified in the sense that it fails to express his subjectivity. This is because the activity of specialized production violates the conditions under which an integral personality or a homogeneous subjective culture is possible.

The division of labor is also responsible for the objectification of the social relations of consumption. The proliferation of cultural forms creates an expanding universe of cultural artifacts. In considering how the relationship between objectification and the division of labor is expressed in the consumption of cultural artifacts, Simmel stresses two theses. First, mass production requires the standardization of cultural artifacts, which must be subjectively indifferent and indiscriminate. Unless this condition is satisfied, the products of mass production can not be accessible to an indefinitely large number of potential consumers. Second, the proliferation of cultural artifacts is possible only because of the standardization of consumption. This means that the consumer of the uniform products of an advanced division of labor must violate the conditions for the integrity of his own subjective culture. These conditions require that he incorporate the artifacts of objective culture into his life only to the extent that their consumption expresses his individuality. However, consumption of the artifacts of mass production is possible only if the differential conditions for the individuality of each consumer are eliminated. The mass-produced commodity no longer molds the unique personality of the consumer. On the contrary, the processes of objectification and the division of labor transform subjective culture in the following respect: The objectified world of cultural forms and their artifacts, the products of mass production, create a new pseudo-subjective culture in which the personality of any given consumer is qualitatively indistinguishable from that of any other.

Differences between consumers are only a consequence of differences in the quantity of cultural artifacts they can consume. This is tantamount to the destruction of the conditions for the possibility of subjective culture.

OBJECTIFICATION, MASCULINITY, AND FEMININITY

Simmel argues that there is an essential connection between the process of objectification and the male character. There are two respects in which objective culture is thoroughly masculine, one more contingent and superficial, the other more profound and definitive for the relationship between objectivity and masculinity. First, objective culture is overwhelmingly a product of male activity. With the exception of the bourgeois household, the artifacts of culture represent the objectification of the male spirit. In Simmel's view, this is a consequence of the relationship between objectification, the division of labor, and the male existence. Recall that objectification depends upon the division of labor and is impossible without it. Every phase of this process depends upon a corresponding level of the division of labor. But as Simmel claims in the essay "The Relative and the Absolute in the Problem of the Sexes," the male is the being that is determined by and for the division of labor: for the division of labor in the sense that the essential features of his character make the man more amenable to the specialization of functions than the woman; by the division of labor in the sense that the process of specialization and the progressive objectification of culture with which it is linked are the definitive forces that mold and transform his character. As a result, "the division of labor is incomparably more congruent with the male nature than with the female." This is the more profound relationship between the objectification of culture and the male existence: Through the medium of the division of labor, there is an elective affinity between objectification and masculinity.

But why should this be the case? Why is there a certain inevitability to the fact that objective culture bears a male stamp? And why is there a lack of congruence or perhaps even a conflict between objectification and femininity? Simmel's answers to these questions lie in his attempt to trace the fundamental differences between the male and the female character, differences which establish that the woman's life resists expression in the artifacts of objective culture for the same reasons that the man's life is predisposed in this direction. The ensuing essays identify five of these basic differences.

SPECIALIZATION/UNIFORMITY

The man can engage in activities that are neither expressions of his life nor integrated into his personality. Moreover, he can do this without threatening the coherence of his identity. As Simmel puts it, the man is not "torn apart by a specialized performance that entails no inherent psychic unity." This does not seem to hold true for the woman. In this respect, her conduct is more homogeneous than the man's and more intimately linked with her character. The reasoning that Simmel uses to support this difference is, of course, somewhat banal and hardly persuasive. He argues that although the division of labor has reduced the former unity of the household—presumably by radically diminishing its importance as a center for the production of goods and services and retaining it as nothing more than a locus for consumption—the activity of the housewife still remains less specialized than any male occupation. This apparently suggests to Simmel that the woman cannot be incorporated into the division of labor without jeopardizing the uniformity of her personal life.

DETACHMENT/INTEGRATION

The psychological condition responsible for the man's predisposition for the division of labor lies in the way he experiences the activity of specialization. It is not an expression of "the private existence of his subjective life." On the contrary, he confronts it in a purely objective fashion, as detached from his own personality. Otherwise his personal existence would indeed be fragmented in a reified and instrumentalized culture. The forms of this culture, increasingly heterogeneous, complex, and remote from the interests and values of his life, would defy his powers of synthesis. The woman lacks this capacity for detachment. An action that does not threaten the integrity of her being seems to be possible for a woman only if it expresses her character. This is because the "periphery" of the female existence "is more closely connected with its center" than holds true for the man. This is also why the woman does not have the ability to detach specialized activities from her identity. It follows that specialization would inevitably tear her personal existence apart. As a result, although the activity of the man can be subordinated to a highly differentiated division of labor without compromising his existence as a male, this is not possible for a woman without destroying the conditions for her existence as a female.[15]

DEPERSONALIZATION/PERSONALIZATION

The man is also capable of insulating his relationships with others from his character. "The man differentiates his total personality from the individual relationship in which he finds himself. He experiences this relationship in a purely objective fashion, detached from all factors that are external to it." The woman, on the other hand, experiences her relationships in an irreducibly personal fashion that is inseparable from her being as a woman. Simmel also links the alleged vulnerability of women to this difference. A woman is more sensitive and more easily offended, not because she is the weaker sex, more fragile and delicate than a man but rather because of her disposition to personalize her relationships. Thus criticism of any aspect of her conduct bears upon her entire person. Because the woman personalizes her life so completely, it follows that she cannot objectify her conduct in forms that are independent of her personal qualities and her identity as a female.[16]

MEDIACY/IMMEDIACY

The woman expresses her subjective states more directly and spontaneously than the man. The expression of male subjective states

15. It is also worth noting how Simmel links the antithetical capacities for detachment and integration to male and female sexuality in the essay "The Relative and the Absolute in the Problem of the Sexes." As an aspect of character that is independent of the woman's relationship to men, female sexuality is "*immanently* defined." This is why "the woman lives in the most profound identity of being and being-a-woman." The distinctive sexuality of the male, on the other hand, is contingent and relational rather than absolute. Since it is completely determined by his relationship to women, "his absolute is not bound up with his sexual being." In spite of the fact that a man's erotic experiences may drive him to madness or suicide, "he feels they are of no significance to what concerns him most deeply."

16. In "Female Culture," Simmel also links the woman's personalization of her relationships to virtues that are conventionally regarded as distinctively feminine: fidelity and constancy.

tends to be oblique and mediated by the forms of objective culture. As a result, women, unlike men, "do not translate their activity into an objective entity that continues to exist independent of that activity." That is because such a translation would destroy the immediacy of the relationship between experience and its expression. This is the most profound reason, or so Simmel claims, "why women generally fail in the creation of objective culture."

BECOMING/BEING

The chief virtue of a man is to act, to achieve or signify something. This means that he is always in a condition of flux, a state of restless becoming that "demands release in objectified activity." As Simmel puts it: "The man externalizes himself. His energy is discharged in his performance. Thus he 'signifies' something that is in some sense independent of him," something that can be realized only in the artifacts of objective culture. The chief virtue of a woman, on the other hand, is to exist in a state of harmonious and self-contained repose, a condition that would be destroyed by its objectification and fragmentation in the forms of culture.

THE PROBLEM OF FEMINISM

As Simmel conceives it, the problem of feminism is a consequence of this intractability of the female character to the division of labor and the process of objectification. In light of the uniformity, integration, personalization, and immediacy of the woman's being and its resistance to any force that threatens its self-contained existence, are there any circumstances under which the objectification of her life is possible? And, if so, what impact would this have upon culture? This is the Simmelian problem of feminism, the question of the presuppositions and consequences of the objectification of women or the feminization of culture.

In the introductory remarks to the essay "Female Culture," Simmel notes that at the beginning of the modern women's movement, the interest of feminism was confined to the domain of subjective culture. The problem was to expand and enrich the personal culture of women by eliminating constraints upon their access to the forms of objective culture. "Insofar as women proposed to move into the forms of life and achievements of men, for them the question concerned their personal participation in cultural goods that already exist and to which they had only been denied access." This is not the issue that concerns Simmel. The Simmelian problem of feminism does not turn on whether women can reproduce the forms of existing objective culture—whether, for example, women can perform up to the standards of men as board chairmen or prime ministers, astronauts or opera conductors. This sort of performance would not qualify as the objectification of the female existence or as the creation of a distinctively female culture. It therefore has no bearing on what Simmel calls the question of "the fundamental relations of the female nature to objective culture." In the relationship between the women's movement and modern culture, the crucial issue is "whether qualitatively new entities and an expansion of the objective content of culture can arise from this movement, the question not only of a multiplication or reproduction of what already exists but rather of creation as well," a creation in which the female character is expressed in cultural artifacts.[17]

In Simmel's time, there were three basic models of the relationship between women and culture.

THE SEPARATE-SPHERES MODEL

In response to the feminist movements of the mid-nineteenth century, the exclusion of women from the rights and statuses of the liberal state that were open to men was elevated to a principle and elaborated as an ideology that explained and legitimated the position that men and women necessarily occupy distinct, mutually exclusive, and noninterchangeable spheres of life. In the interest of brevity and simplicity, this model may be reduced to four interdependent doctrines.

The market/home dichotomy. The model reserved all nondomestic economic production for men. Ideally, the woman was even dis-

17. The Simmelian problem of feminism may also be linked to the question of the possibility of a feminist politics of culture: By means of objectification of the woman's existence, is an advanced objective culture possible that does not trace the apparently inevitable path that leads from reification and instrumentalization to the fragmentation of individual existence? In other words, is there a distinctively female mode of objectification which would ensure the development of objective culture without destroying the coherence and integrity of subjective culture?

charged from all domestic production with the exception of child-bearing and the general surveillance of household affairs. In the ideal home, all chores, including cleaning, producing for domestic consumption, and childcare, were performed by servants under the directions of the mistress of the house.[18]

The public/private dichotomy. It follows that the male and female members of a family were separated during the working day. Men went to places of employment and civic activity. Boys went to school, where they were trained to assume these public responsibilities. Women—without the right to take up a vocation, vote, hold political office, or pursue an education that would enable them to participate in public political and economic life—remained at home, where the wife supervised the household, saw to the education of her daughters, did charitable work, and visited the homes of her peers. The purpose of female education was to develop domestic and interpersonal skills rather than to acquire intellectual competence or professional training. The young woman learned the traditional techniques of household management either from her mother or from practical manuals. She acquired social graces, drawing-room etiquette, and some facility in dancing and playing keyboard instruments either in private schools or from tutors. However, it was

18. Since women of the lower classes obviously could not satisfy the conditions of the model if they were employed at menial tasks in the homes of other women, it is clear that this ideal required a socioeconomic status that made the employment of a staff of servants possible. Historically it seems to have been the dominant model for women of the middle or bourgeois classes. Because the male aristocrat typically lived off the income of rent or other investments, neither he nor his wife engaged in economic production outside the home. Thus the differences between his life and hers were not so great as those that separated the middle-class man from his wife. Although the model was a preeminently bourgeois ethic, it was also understood as the ideal to which the working classes should aspire and, insofar as possible, approximate or at least imitate. For recent work on the separate-spheres model, see Burstyn (1980), McMillan (1981), and Smith (1981). Concerning the premises that were to support the separate-spheres model in American intellectual life during the late nineteenth and early twentieth centuries, see Rosenberg (1982), especially chapter 1, where the role of these premises in the resistance to higher education for women is discussed. In the arguments against female suffrage, the ultimate issue at stake was the legitimacy of the separate-spheres model. The relationship between the extension of the franchise to women and the acceptability of this model is quite explicit in Harrison (1978). See especially chapter 4.

believed that an education in discursive reasoning and the mastery of the instrumental rationalities governing the polity and the economy would corrupt woman's innate, intuitive judgment, compromise her femininity, and thus render her incapable of fulfilling her natural functions as a wife and mother (Burstyn 1980, pp. 36–39).

The production/consumption dichotomy. The home, the woman's place, was the locus of consumption. The few productive activities that were performed there, such as the preparation of food, were intended for domestic consumption. This ideal of the woman as the specialist in consumption and the home as the site of this specialization became possible only in the phase of industrialization that detached the production of goods and services from the household and concentrated it in special workshops or factories.

Ethical dualism. The separate-spheres model imposed an ethic of charity, chastity, and sacrifice upon women. While men conquered the public worlds of power and the marketplace, women were expected to perform services for their families and engage in charitable activities for those less fortunate. The psychology that ascribed acquisitiveness, emotional reserve, cool rationality, authority, and decisiveness to men and charity, self-sacrifice, emotionality, submissiveness, and a delicate sensibility to women obviously imposed a double standard of morality upon the sexes. It was perhaps most unambiguous in the domain of sexual ethics. Although chastity was required of daughters and fidelity demanded from wives, premarital sexual activity for young men and extramarital liaisons for husbands did not have the same morally pejorative status.

The separate-spheres model confined the participation of women in objective culture to the household. In his fascinating discussion of the home as a cultural form in which all of the contents of life may be structured—a fundamental category on the basis of which the entire world of culture can be constructed and experienced—Simmel claims that the household is in fact the only area of culture where the woman's life has been successfully objectified. In essence, the home is "the supreme cultural achievement of women" because it is the only cultural achievement of women, the only cultural form that has made the expression of the female existence possible without fragmenting, and thereby destroying, its homogeneity. This is because the properties of the home—its unity and completeness, and the personal and intimate quality of domestic life—reproduce the basic qualities of the woman's life on the level of objective culture.[19]

The exclusion of women from the public domain of culture was based on a complex set of motives, and the separate-spheres model made use of several different varieties of argument. Among them, sociological, economic, psychological, anatomical, gynecological, and theological considerations can be identified.[20]

Discussion of public affairs by women, especially in the household, would compromise the authority of the husband and father and jeopardize the structure of the family. Entry into the public sphere, especially through higher education, would make some women discontented and argumentative wives. In other cases, sexual license would be encouraged, and women would be led to abandon marriage altogether. In either instance, the institutions of marriage and the family would be endangered. If women entered the job market, numerous undesirable consequences were expected to follow. Husbands, homes, and children would be neglected. The women themselves would become defeminized, and their health would be threatened. A surplus of labor would be created, as a result of which wages would fall. Since employers typically paid women workers lower wages, men would be driven out of work and families would be deprived of support.

The psychology of the female character encouraged the belief that women were intuitive and emotional creatures, unable to detach passion from judgment, unfit for assessing the consequences of alternative measures in an impersonal way, and incapable of discursive thought and the practice of following long chains of logic. It

---

19. This conception of the symmetry between the home and the woman's existence is, of course, a highly questionable thesis. Consider, for example, the old proto-feminism implicit in Ibsen's tragedies of high-bourgeois domesticity. In *A Doll's House, Hedda Gabler, The Master Builder,* and *Rosmersholm,* the home is a moral and psychological prison or a psychopathic ward. Or consider the new feminism of the contemporary affluent middle classes, which represents the home as the locus of the depoliticization and privatization of the woman, the instrument of her domination by the male world, and the basis of her reduction as housewife to an appendage of the home itself.

20. There is a useful summary of these arguments in Burstyn 1980, chapters 2–6.

follows that they were mentally unqualified for the responsibilities of the public sphere and the instrumental reasoning essential to economic and political activity.

Following the work of Darwin, it was argued that men and women evolved at different rates and with quite different results. Cranial measurements and the determination of brain volume suggested to Victorian anatomists that the male brain was both larger and more highly developed than the female. This led to the conclusion that men were innately more intelligent than women. In addition, the delicate physiology of the woman's reproductive system made it impossible for her to withstand the pressures of higher education and the stress of competition without endangering her health and reproductive capacity and ultimately risking sterility. If higher education, a job, and public responsibility made women sterile, this would, of course, transform the basis of their relationship to men. As a result, the structure of society would be altered in unimaginable and undesirable ways.

Finally, the authority of Genesis shows that God intended woman to be man's helper and subordinate. The circumstances surrounding the Fall—Eve's deception and her temptation of Adam—demonstrated the woman's defective judgment and moral inferiority. Her subsequent punishment by God—pain in childbirth and obedience to the will of her husband—required humility, restraint, self-denial, and sacrifice. Thus the Christian woman was obliged to submit to her husband, just as she submits to God.

THE LIBERAL MODEL

The assumptions of the separate-spheres ideal remained relatively diffuse and inarticulate until they were called into question. That occurred when the feminist movements of the late nineteenth century attacked this ideal on the basis of the liberal model. In Germany, the main source for the liberal model was John Stuart Mill's famous essay "On the Subjection of Woman" (1869), which was widely read and became extremely influential.[21] On the liberal model, the natural

---

21. For recent work in English on the German feminism of the Wilhelmian period, see Thönnessen (1973), Evans (1976), Hackett (1976a, 1976b), Kaplan (1977, 1979), and Quataert (1979).

creative capacities of men and women are the same. Thus their innate abilities to contribute to the forms of objective culture and to create cultural artifacts should also be the same. This means that the principles governing access to objective culture by men should apply to women as well. It follows that the problem of feminism can be resolved by eliminating the constraints upon the woman's free access to such forms of culture as the law, politics, the economy, and education. To put this in another way, women deserve what men already have: the same cultural rights and the same access to the production of cultural artifacts. Since their ability to contribute to objective culture is the same, there should also be an equal distribution of rights to make that contribution.

If the liberal state is the political organization that defines, legitimizes, and enforces these rights, and if the liberal order is the set of institutions within which the liberal state functions, then liberal feminism amounts to the extension of the male statuses of the liberal order—the various interlinked rights of citizenship, the franchise, legal equality, the ownership of property, education, political office, and equal access to the labor market—to women. Thus it represents a quantitative expansion of the objective culture of the liberal order to include women.

As Mill argues, the principle that regulates the relations between the sexes should be "perfect equality, admitting no power or privilege on one side, nor disability on the other" (Rossi 1970, p. 125). This requires granting women "the free use of their faculties, by leaving them the free choice of their employments, and opening to them the same field of occupation and the same prizes and encouragements as to other human beings" (Rossi 1970, pp. 220–21). As a result, "women in general would be brought up equally capable of understanding business, public affairs, and the higher matters of speculation, with men in the same class of society; and the select few of the one as well as of the other sex, who were qualified not only to comprehend what is done or thought by others, but to think or do something considerable themselves, would meet with the same facilities for improving and training their capacities in the one sex as in the other" (Rossi 1970, pp. 221–22).

As regards the basic assumption of the separate-spheres model, that women have a distinctive nature which excludes them from the male worlds of economic production and public responsibility, Mill claims that we have no reason to believe that there are any fundamental or qualitative differences in character and capacities between men and women who are able to enjoy the free use of their faculties. However, he introduces the reservation that a wife with children in a family that depends upon an income from wages or salary should probably not take up employment outside the home. This restriction upon the freedom of the wife and mother seems to be based on two considerations. First, if she bears and rears the children and manages the affairs of the household, she is already doing more than her fair share. In addition, the pursuit of extra-domestic activities would probably compromise her ability to meet these responsibilities. Mill compares the woman's decision to marry with the man's choice of a profession: It imposes a primary set of obligations, requiring the renunciation of all enterprises inconsistent with their fulfillment.

Nevertheless, Mill also makes it clear that this is not an absolute moral principle governing the relations between marriage partners but simply a prudent rule of thumb: "the utmost latitude ought to exist for the adaptation of general rules to individual suitabilities" (Rossi 1970, p. 179). In other words, nothing should stand in the way of the woman who is capable of pursuing other occupations at the same time that she sees to the fulfillment of her domestic responsibilities. This reservation is not a consequence of the liberal feminist doctrine. It is, rather, an expression of Mill's personal traditionalism—or perhaps his lack of sociological imagination—in matters concerning the conjugal division of labor. At most, it is an indication of his residual acceptance of certain consequences of the separate-spheres model, in spite of the fact that he rejected the premises on which they are based.

THE SOCIALIST MODEL

The third basic model of the relationshp between women and culture influential in Simmel's time was socialist feminism. The socialist model embraces the basic ideal of liberalism and its solution to the problem of feminism: equal access by women to the forms of culture. However, there are three important respects in which it rejects the liberal model. First, access to the forms of culture is not regarded as equivalent to the rights of the liberal state; as a consequence of the general principles of socialism, socialist feminism denies women the liberal right to the ownership of private property as well as other rights which depend upon it. Second, the socialist model holds that women cannot achieve access to the forms of culture within the limits of the liberal state. This is because the oppression of women is an essential aspect or an inevitable consequence of the liberal order. There are two reasons why this is the case: the patriarchal quality of the liberal order, as a consequence of which women are inevitably dominated by men; and the exploitative quality of the liberal order, as a consequence of which the working classes, male and female, are inevitably exploited by the propertied classes. Thus the liberal state cannot satisfy its own demand of rights for women. In this sense, liberal feminism is self-contradictory. It postulates an ideal condition the nonfulfillment of which is ensured by its own principles. Its ultimate value cannot be attained because of the nature of the liberal state itself. Therefore socialist feminism agrees with the liberal model on the point that the conditions for the liberation of women are the same as those for men: The emancipation of women is human emancipation. However, it rejects the view that these conditions can be met within the liberal social order. Finally, this is the basis of the third fundamental difference between liberal and socialist feminism. It is why the socialist model requires the transformation of the liberal order. Because the oppression of women cannot be eliminated within the parameters of the liberal state, genuine female emancipation—a social order in which there are no restrictions upon the access of women to the forms of culture—depends upon a revolution that will replace this order. Thus the socialist model requires the transformation of the female statuses of the liberal state in accordance with the aims of socialism. It is a consequence of the general doctrines of a socialist politics of culture, in the same sense that the liberal model is a consequence of the general doctrines of a liberal politics of culture.

The single most important text in the development of socialist feminism was undoubtedly August Bebel's *Women under Socialism*,

originally published in 1883.[22] Although Bebel shares Mill's general
liberal feminist aims—"the complete emancipation of woman and
her equality with man" (Bebel 1971, p. 349)—he argues that this is
impossible in the liberal state or "Class-State," which sanctions the
exploitation of the working class by the propertied class and the
closely related domination of women by men.[23] Thus consider the
liberal movement of civil rights for women, which Bebel describes
as "a Sisyphus work" that is "done with as much noise as possible, to
the end of deceiving oneself and others on the score of the necessity
for radical change" (Bebel 1971, p. 142). Even if this movement
succeeds, "nothing is thereby changed in the total condition of the
sex" (Bebel 1971, p. 4).

There are two reasons why this is the case. First, although liberal
feminism might reduce the economic and social dependence of
women upon men, it would not eliminate it altogether. Second and
more important, it would not eliminate the economic dependence

22. *Die Frau und der Sozialismus*. The current English edition (Bebel 1971) is a
reprint of the execrable 1904 translation by Daniel de Leon. Neither the English nor
the German title is an accurate indication of the contents of the book, which deals
mainly with the variety of historical conditions for the oppression and exploitation of
women, especially in capitalist societies. In spite of its enormous influence, Bebel's
book has been curiously ignored in the recent Anglo-American feminist literature. For
example, in her introduction to a collection of essays on the equality of the sexes by
John Stuart Mill and Harriet Taylor Mill, Alice Rossi claims that "The Subjection of
Women" "almost stands alone as an intellectual analysis of the position of women and
an appeal for political action to secure equality of the sexes" (Rossi 1970, p. 4).
Charlotte Perkins Gilman's *Women and Economics* (1898) and Simone de Beauvoir's
The Second Sex (1951) are named as the only comparable undertakings. Mill is also
identified as "the solitary male intellectual figure" to produce an analysis of the
conditions for the subjection of women comparable to liberal and radical analyses of
other oppressed groups (Rossi 1970, p. 5). Both of these claims are, of course, false. It
should also be noted that Bebel's political advocacy of equality for women was more
uncompromising than Mill's, and his analysis of the conditions responsible for the
oppression of women was more systematic, comprehensive, and detailed.

23. See Bebel 1971, p. 233. At this point, Bebel comes quite close to the idea that
women constitute a social class that is defined by sex. However, it is obvious that he
cannot accept this idea and its consequences, for that would require the rejection of
socialist feminism. If women as a class are victims of exploitation, and if this class is
sexually defined, then the exploitation of women will clearly not be eliminated by a
socialist revolution. Regardless of how radical its aims pretend to be, socialism does
not propose to abolish female sexuality.

that the working woman shares with the working man. This is why the general aims of liberal feminism require the transformation of the liberal social order, "to the end that both wage slavery, under which the working woman deeply pines, and sex slavery, which is intimately connected with our property and industrial systems, be wiped out" (Bebel 1971, p. 4). The aims of liberal feminism cannot be realized by the liberal state because of the intimate link between the sexual domination of women and the capitalist expropriation of wage labor, both of which are legitimized by the private-property system of the liberal order. For this reason, "a radical transformation of society" is necessary which will create the conditions for "the real economic and spiritual independence of both sexes."[24]

SIMMELIAN FEMINISM

Each of these three models of the relationship between women and culture can be called reductionist in the sense that none of them acknowledges the autonomy of femininity as a form of life which structures human experience on the basis of its own distinctive principles. The separate-spheres model subordinates femininity to motherhood and the family—and, at least in the case of Wilhelmian Germany, to the national interest or the fatherland as well. The liberal and socialist models are reductionist in the sense that they derive feminist ideals and values from the basic political assumptions of liberalism or socialism. From the perspective of each model, being a woman is a contingent or derivative status that depends upon some other condition. In the separate-spheres model, being a woman is being a wife and mother. In the liberal and socialist models, being a woman is grounded in an egalitarian philosophical anthropology according to which the cultural status of women is basically the same as that of men.[25]

24. Bebel 1971, p. 5. See also pp. 144–45, 181–82, 342–49. Versions of the socialist model in the recent Anglo-American literature include Mitchell (1971, 1974), Rowbotham (1972, 1973), and Eisenstein (1979, 1981).

25. In Eisenstein 1981, there are two basic confusions concerning the general relationship between liberalism and feminism. First, it is maintained that "all feminism is liberal at its root in that the universal feminist claim that woman is an independent being (from man) is premised on the eighteenth century liberal concep-

This is the fundamental reason why Simmel cannot accept these models. In his view, human experience is defined and molded by a plurality of forms of life that are independent and irreducibly different from one another. Being a woman is one of these forms of life. This anti-reductionist turn of Simmel's thought is based on a variety of closely related considerations: a critique of the Enlightenment theory of rationality as a set of unified theoretical and practical laws of reason that apply to all experience in the same way; an ontology of human experience that is committed to the view that human life cannot be reduced to any single form; an epistemology that stresses the plurality of radically different and incommensurable modes of knowledge; and a conception of modernity which holds that the variety of forms of life is threatened by the progressive "mechanization" of human experience in the money economy and the relentless "intellectualization" of life produced by the dominant form of modern culture, scientific rationality.

In the development of this anti-reductionist tendency of Simmel's thought, his interpretation of the unique cultural significance of Kant's philosophy occupies a preeminent position, for it is in the work of Kant that the project of the intellectualization of life receives its most sublime expression.[26] At the beginning of his book on Kant and Goethe (1906), Simmel presents an account of the medieval synthesis of man and nature that resolved the oppositions between

tion of the independent and autonomous self" (p. 4). This thesis holds true only for liberal feminism. It cannot be extended to any form of socialist feminism that rejects the liberal conception of individual autonomy, nor can it cover a Simmelian feminism which rejects the liberal philosophical anthropology and its assumption that masculinity and femininity entail no fundamental cultural differences. Second, it is also maintained that all feminism is "radically feminist" in the sense that the woman's identity is defined by her membership in a sexual class (p. 4). In that case, liberal feminism cannot be radical. Liberalism rejects the view that sexual criteria are relevant to the cultural identity of the person. As persons, both men and women have the same essential cultural attributes. It follows that any respect in which women constitute a sexual class will be irrelevant to the liberal conception of women. To put this in another way, to accept the view of women as defined by their membership in a sexual class is to reject liberal feminism. Therefore it cannot be true that all feminism is radical in this sense.

26. See Simmel 1921, pp. 6–7, 9–10, 21–22, 107, 111–12, 116–17, 158–59.

God and man, spirit and flesh, and value and nature, dichotomies that were generated by the most fundamental assumptions of Christian culture. The Renaissance, however, destroyed the intellectual framework on which this synthesis was based and created the need for a new ensemble of forms and a new synthesis of the contents of life. Early modern culture responded to this predicament by producing a new set of absolute dichotomies: man and nature, subject and object, mind and body. The definitive cultural problem of the eighteenth century was the reconciliation of these oppositions, the problem of re-establishing the fractured unity of nature and spirit.

Simmel's interpretation of Kant turns on the revolutionary role he ascribes to Kant's work in the consummation of this new cultural synthesis. In the Kantian conception of the world, nature no longer contains the slightest trace of mind or spirit. A complete science of nature is a mathematicized mechanics. Spirit, on the other hand, functions according to completely different laws that are immanent to the spirit itself. It follows that nature as the kingdom of necessity and the human world of spirit as the kingdom of freedom do not intersect. The audacity of Kant's achievement lies in the fact that he unified these two apparently juxtaposed and incommensurable domains in an integrated weltanschauung, which in its finished state represents the apotheosis of the "scientific-intellectualistic" conception of the world, "the supreme triumph of intellectuality" (Simmel 1921, p. 117). As Simmel understands it, the definitive aim of the Kantian project of intellectualization is to provide an exhaustive conception of the world within the limits of one form. The contents of life are represented insofar as they can be conceived by reference to the a priori categories of the understanding. *Nomos*, the idea of a lawlike regularity and necessity imposed by the intellect, is the axiomatic concept of this project.

Simmel interprets Kant's thought as an attempt to establish that the norms which are valid for the domain of thought also govern every province of life. Consider the domains of natural science, natural religion, liberal economics, the politics of revolution, and the ethics of the categorical imperative. Each of these provinces of culture is based on the assumption that the world is governed by universal and invariant principles that entail a ruthless and rigorous consistency, the axiomatization and systematization of the most diverse phenomena, the elimination of all forms of subjective affect, the reduction of quality to quantity, and the incorporation of the total universe of human experience into a domain of cultural artifacts that is equally accessible to everyone and, in this sense, is objective and impartial. The result is the complete intellectualization of the world, which becomes intelligible insofar as it is reduced to laws that are prescribed by the understanding: natural laws according to which the external or material world functions, and moral laws according to which the inner or spiritual world is subject. However, there is an important sense in which both the natural law and the moral law can be derived from the same principles. This is because both are determined by the a priori categories of the understanding. These categories constitute the space in which all contents are comprehended within the limits of a single form: that of scientific intellectuality. Although the autonomous will of Kant's moral philosophy is the exclusive source of significance and value, the morality of volition is itself determined by reference to a logical norm. According to Simmel, this philosophical move exhibits "the most extreme and subtle triumph of conceptual and logical intellectuality." It betrays a "logical fanaticism which attempts to impose the form of mathematical clarity and precision upon the totality of life" (Simmel 1921, p. 7). In the execution of this synthesis, therefore, Kant becomes the most radical exponent of the modern scientific spirit.

Simmel claims that this form of intellectuality is the cultural synthesis that has dominated the West for three centuries. Its paramount status is demonstrated by the importance ascribed to science in the modern world, exhibited not merely in the actual progress of science and its results, but above all in the commitment to the cultural project of science: the belief that there is some sense in which life would be consummate or perfect if it were governed by a complete and perfected science.

From the perspective of Simmel's metaphysics, the Kantian project of intellectualization violates the heterogeneity of life. Simmel's rejection of Kant's position is a consequence of his repudiation of one of the fundamental premises of the liberal conception of the world, which is not limited to a politics but also includes an ethics, a conception of the nature of man, society, and history, a theory of knowledge, and a metaphysics as well.[27] Liberalism is committed to what might be called an axiom of universal commensurability: All forms of life are commensurable with one another in the sense that they can all be understood and judged on the basis of the same principles. Hobbes's conception of a politics based on a science of man; Locke's conception of a law of nature that governs not only the physical world of bodies in motion but also the moral world of conflicting interests; the insistence of Voltaire and Hume that religious beliefs should be subjected to the same critical standards that govern scientific beliefs; Bentham's derivation of the principles of ethics and law from those of psychology; John Stuart Mill's conception of a moral science grounded in the methods of natural science; the ideology of the American and the French revolutions and their commitment to an egalitarian philosophical anthropology; liberal feminism together with its offspring, socialist feminism, and their commitment to the view that there are no fundamental cultural differences between the male and the female character—all these ideas are based on this axiom, which in Simmel's view received its consummate and most systematic elaboration in the thought of Kant.[28]

In Simmel's thought, the incommensurability of different cultural forms is a consequence of irreducible differences in the energies and interests of life itself. History, politics, ethics, law, and religion are not reducible to science, nor is any one of these forms reducible to any of the others. As we learn in the essay "On Love," the experience of love cannot be explained as a consequence of more elementary phenomena or reconstructed from the concomitant interaction of such phenomena. A "rationalistic psychology" cannot succeed in reducing love to egoism or altruism or some compound of the two, nor can love be derived from a relationship between sentiment and sensuality. As Simmel puts it, love cannot be constructed "from a plurality of factors none of which is love itself." The same considerations hold for flirtation. Although it is intimately linked with sensual-

---

27. The analysis of liberalism as an exhaustive weltanschauung is perhaps the chief merit of Roberto Mangabeira Unger's *Knowledge and Politics* (1975).

28. Simmel develops his critique of Kantian intellectualization in his interpretations of Goethe and Nietzsche. See especially *Kant und Goethe* (1906), *Schopenhauer und Nietzsche* (1923b; original edition, 1907), and *Goethe* (1913).

ity, play, and art, it cannot be represented as a derivative compound of these factors. And as Simmel argues in the essays "Female Culture" and "The Relative and the Absolute in the Problem of the Sexes," femininity cannot be reductively analyzed either. A woman's existence is fundamentally different from a man's. It is constituted on the basis of its own immanent principles, which generate a distinctive form of life. This form of life cannot be derived from any relationship in which the woman happens to find herself, such as her relationship to a man; nor can it be reduced to a status that defines femininity in terms of the woman's relations to others, such as that of wife, mother, or daughter.

Because the three models of the relationship between women and culture fail to acknowledge the autonomy of femininity, they do not address the problem of feminism as Simmel conceives it. The essays that follow—above all the study of "Female Culture"—trace two mutually inconsistent responses to this problem. Neither is presented or supported in any detail. On the contrary, both represent no more than the most cursory of sketches, documenting the famous Simmelian reserve, ambivalence, and lack of commitment expressed in the refusal to defend a position that would resolve the issue between alternative, internally consistent and plausible, and yet inconclusive solutions to the same problem.

On the one hand, Simmel entertains the possibility of a feminist response to the problem of the relationship between women and culture. In this view, the energies and interests of the woman's life are objectified on the basis of the distinctive givens of the female existence. This response is essential if the virtually complete male domination of objective culture is to be eliminated. "The naive conflation of male values with values as such can give way only if the female existence as such is acknowledged as having a basis fundamentally different from the male." Thus it is imperative to recognize "two existential totalities," a male culture and a female culture, "each structured according to a completely autonomous rule."

On the other hand, Simmel offers only the most insubstantial of suggestions concerning how such a female culture might be possible and the conditions it would have to satisfy. Consider, for example, the extended discussion in "Female Culture" devoted to the question of whether women are able to create artifacts of objective culture that men cannot produce. This is presumably intended as an account of the sorts of qualities an autonomous female culture might conceivably exhibit. Here Simmel discusses—in an extremely adumbrated, vague, and speculative way—the unique contributions that women have made or might make to medicine, the historical sciences, poetry, mathematics, the novel, the dance, the plastic arts, and acting. But even if all the claims made in this section are sound, it does not follow that these allegedly unique contributions to objective culture qualify as expressions of femininity: the homogeneity and integration, personalization and immediacy of existence which, in Simmel's view, define the essence of the female mode of life.

Moreover, this entire discussion is compromised by Simmel's failure to distinguish two questions that are logically independent and may have quite different answers. What can women contribute to objective culture that men cannot? And can culture be feminized in the sense that certain cultural forms would qulaify as objectifications of the woman's existence? There are some contexts in which it is not clear whether Simmel's discussion is limited to the first question or includes the second as well. In the final analysis, we are left with some fascinating allusions to the possibility of a distinctive female mode of medical diagnosis and historical interpretation based on the assumption that "a different form of knowledge is based on a different mode of being"; the speculation that "the distinctive relationship to space suggested in the gestures of women would have to be objectified in distinctively female works of art"; and the intriguing but purely conjectural idea that the objectification of the female nature might lead to the discovery of "a new continent of culture." However, Simmel obviously does not fancy himself as the explorer of this new continent, nor does he even attempt to trace the outlines of its geography.

Is that perhaps because the undiscovered continent of female culture does not exist? This is the second response to the the problem of feminism that Simmel considers, his skeptical resolution of the question. In light of the record of contributions that women have made to objective culture—from mathematics and medicine to the dance and the plastic arts—"no one," Simmel claims, "will deny that individual women succeed or can succeed in creating artifacts of objective culture." But this consideration does not settle the question of whether it is the female character that is objectified in these artifacts. Indeed, it is irrelevant to this question. Simmel suspects that the problem of whether the woman's existence is in fact expressed in any artifact of culture, with the sole exception of the home, "cannot be answered with complete certainty." This reflection leads him to consider why this might be the case. The answer may not lie in the contingencies of objective culture—for example, the fact that specific provinces of culture at given stages of their development may be more or less resistant or unsuited to the cultural creativity of women. On the contrary, it may lie in a more fundamental conflict between objective culture and the female mode of life.

This conflict seems to be a consequence of two distinctive properties of femininity. The first could be called an aspect of the metaphysics of the female character. The contents of the woman's life are not defined and molded on the basis of the subjectivity/objectivity dichotomy that is essential to the process of culture. Simmel claims that the woman's existence lies beyond this dichotomy. It forms the contents of life as a direct expression of its energies and interests, independent of the mediation of cultural forms. These forms are possible only on the basis of norms that hold independent of the persons to whom they apply. In this sense, they are detached from subjective culture, and thus they presuppose the subjectivity/objectivity dichotomy. However, the female mode of life cannot be subjected to these autonomous norms without destroying its distinctive qualities. This is why it cannot be governed by the subjectivity/objectivity dichotomy. It is also why femininity cannot qualify as a cultural form.

The second property could be called an aspect of the phenomenology of the female character. The contents of the woman's life are experienced not as externalized or detached from experience itself but rather as an immediate and immanent expression of experience. Cultural artifacts, however, are mediated by the forms in which they are produced; they cannot qualify as immediate expressions of life. This means that if the woman's existence can be expressed only in a direct and unmediated fashion, the artifacts in which this existence is realized must be independent of the forms of culture. They cannot qualify as depersonalized entities detached from the woman's experience. It follows that neither the actions that express the female experience nor the artifacts that constitute the products of these expressions—if indeed there are such distinctively female actions and artifacts—can fall within the domain of culture.

Suppose that women neither categorize experience on the basis of the subjectivity/objectivity dichotomy nor experience the contents of life as independent of the experience itself. In that case, it seems that the objectification of the female existence, or the feminization of culture, is impossible. In other words, from these considerations it apparently follows that there is no female culture but rather an autonomous female mode of being irreducible to culture and incommensurable with its forms. Although there may be women who happen to be scientists, judges, prime ministers, or poets, there is no distinctively female science, law, politics, or art. "Under these circumstances," Simmel argues, "the male monopolization of objective culture would persist, but with justification. That is because culture as a formal principle would qualify as a one-sided male principle. Juxtaposed to it, the female form of existence would present itself as a different form, autonomous on the basis of its ultimate essence, incommensurable on the basis of the standards of the male principle, and with contents that are not formed in the same way."

Therefore Simmel's reasoning in this skeptical response to the problem of the relationship between women and culture does not open up the possibility of an alternative female culture, or even the possibility of a more limited feminized counterculture in which certain forms would qualify as objectifications of the woman's life. On the contrary, it requires the idea of a female mode of life that exists as an alternative to culture. It apparently follows that there is no solution to the Simmelian problem of feminism, the question of the conditions for the objectification of the woman's existence. The female mode of being cannot be objectified without being transformed into something else. As Simmel suggests, the idea of a female culture seems to be a contradiction in terms. In that case, there can be no feminist politics of culture. As a result of objectification, the defeminized woman would be disintegrated and depersonalized by the division of labor. In the final analysis, she would share the fate of the man in an increasingly reified and instrumentalized world. Thus it seems that a putatively feminist politics of culture would have one of two possible results. Either it would fail on the grounds that the woman's life cannot be expressed in cultural forms, or it would result in the masculinization of the female character, in which case women would be incorporated into the division of labor and the objectification of culture along with men. In Simmel's view, the latter result would seem to be the ultimate consequence of a liberal or a socialist feminism: the creation of a monosexual culture in which women would first be violated and then transformed as a result of objectification.

In view of these skeptical conclusions concerning the possibility of a female culture, it may not be beside the point to examine the premises on which Simmel bases them: his view of the relationship between life, the female existence, and culture. Two questions are especially important here. First, is there any reason to accept Simmel's supposition of a timeless essence that defines the female character? This issue is, of course, prior to the consideration of whether, given the existence of such an essence, Simmel has correctly identified it in the qualities of homogeneity and integration, personalization and immediacy. Simmel himself, quite true to form in this case, gives no reason at all for this supposition. To limit the question to the sphere of Occidental culture alone, consider the women of Euripides—Iphigenia, Electra, Clytemnestra, Jocasta, and Antigone—the sexual virtuosos of late imperial Rome; the Renaissance princesses of northern Italy; the wives of the early British and American entrepreneurs who worked alongside their husbands; the nineteenth-century women who inspired Thackeray's Rebecca Sharp, Charlotte Brontë's Jane Eyre, and George Eliot's Maggie Tulliver and Dorothea Brooke; female peasants and female members of the urban proletariat; the "new Soviet woman"; not only the women who read *Cosmopolitan* and *Vogue* but also those who read the *Wall Street Journal* and *Foreign Affairs*. They seem to exhibit such an overwhelming variety of qualities which distinguish them from their male contemporaries that it appears rash to suggest that they all have the same underlying female nature. In addition, it is not clear how the conception of a timeless female essence can be reconciled with Simmel's own theory of culture, which posits what might be called a dialectical relationship between human life and forms. Human experience is expressed in forms that generate new existential interests and values. These qualities of life in turn create new forms, which again transform the properties of life. The female existence, along with every other mode of human life, is caught up in this perpetual flux of life and form. This doctrine does not seem to be consistent with the possibility of an unchanging female nature. Indeed, given this conception of the relationship between life and form, only one timeless or essential quality can be ascribed to human life: namely, the disposition to express itself in a variety of changing forms.

This consideration leads to the second question that is important in the present context. Even if there can be no timelessly valid female essence, is a female mode of existence still possible that is not objectified in any form? Simmel's view of the relationship between life and form also seems to eliminate this possibility. If, as Simmel claims, life necessarily realizes its energies and interests in forms that qualify as more-than-life, then it seems that his conception of the female nature is incoherent. Recall that this conception supposes both that the female mode of being is independent of the subjectivity/objectivity dichotomy and also that it is not expressed or externalized in forms that are detached from life. But if human life, which of course includes the life of women, is invariably objectified and externalized in forms, then there can be no female nature in this sense. Thus the problem of feminism cannot turn on the question of whether a mode of life is possible that is not expressed in some form. Simmel's philosophical anthropology excludes this possibility. The issue is, rather, whether there is a medium of objectification—a mode of interaction between life and form—that expresses the distinctive qualities of the woman's existence.

THE PROBLEM OF FEMINISM RECONSIDERED

To raise this question is to return to the Simmelian problem of feminism, the problem of the possibility of a feminized culture. Although the legitimacy of this problem is denied by Simmel's skeptical conception of the relationship between women and culture, this conception is vitiated by his basic ontological assumptions. Indeed, it is inconsistent with the most fundamental premise of Simmel's thought, his doctrine of the relationship between life and form. The undiscovered continent of culture that would be revealed by the objectification of the woman's existence lies on the horizon of this possibility, and perhaps it does not require too much imagination to envision its outlines. There are several possibilities. A female culture could be formed by an ensemble of cultural spheres different from those that define male culture. Or, although the general cultural spheres might be the same, certain characteristically male forms might disappear with the development of new, distinctively female forms. Or cultural forms might be structured on the basis of distinctively female givens or formal principles, with the result that quite different artifacts would be produced. Or the same sorts of artifacts might be produced, but with radically different properties.

As a way of translating these abstract possibilities into the realm of concrete plausibility, we might argue against Simmel's skeptical response to the problem of feminism with materials that he has placed at our disposal. Consider the province of culture that, in Simmel's view, is most conspicuously resistant to feminization. This is law, the area of culture in which we should least expect to find objectified expressions of the female character. Simmel claims that the woman's antagonism to legal institutions seems to result in a peculiarly female antipathy to law. Yet he also reminds us that this does not necessarily amount to an animus against the law itself; perhaps it is only a disposition to reject the reified and instrumentalized male legal culture, "which is the only law we have, and which for this reason seems to us to be the law as such." He even admits, at least as a speculative possibility, the idea of an alternative female "sense of justice" which is independent of the male conception of justice and irreducible to it. Such a female sense of justice, Simmel suggests, is capable of producing its own distinctive body of law. The refusal to acknowledge the independent legitimacy and the immanent validity of this body of law could be defended only by means of a circular logic which presupposes the existing legal system and rejects the possibility of a female jurisprudence on the basis of the principles of justice and the legal norms that in fact obtain.

Suppose we take this purely hypothetical and hastily sketched possibility more seriously than Simmel himself seems to have done. Is there some truth to the idea that, in our culture at least, a characteristically female ethic can be identified, a peculiarly female mode of resolving practical value conflicts? Suppose, as we are sometimes told, that women—or at least the contemporary Occidental women of advanced industrial societies—have a distinctive moral language that imposes a specific construction on moral problems and that, as a result, women speak with a characteristically female voice in settling moral issues.[29] According to this view, the paradigmatic male value judgment abstracts from all the specific contingencies of the issue at stake. Detached from individual needs and social conventions, it is based instead on putatively universal principles of right conduct and justice. As a result, it is possible to reach a thoroughly objective assessment of practical conflicts. The judgment is objective in the sense that it does not depend upon any psychological, historical, or social considerations. This means that the judge decides the case in an impersonal fashion, independent of his own emotions and prejudices and the particular interests and values of the parties to the conflict, even independent of his own moral intuitions concerning what is right and wrong. Thus male justice is formal in the sense that the resolution of practical value conflicts is grounded on universal principles employed according to procedures that apply to every case in the same way, regardless of its individual peculiarities.

The female moral judgment, on the other hand, is emotionally and empathetically grounded in compassion and care. The substance of moral problems is defined not by abstract and hypothetical dilemmas but rather by the concrete moral conflicts that arise in real life. Competing claims and rights are not weighed in the abstract, by reference to their logical, ethical, or legal priority. They are, rather, considered in the light of the concrete and potentially unique characteristics of the conflict, from the perspective of the actual conduct of

29. See Carol Gilligan (1977, 1982). The conclusions of Gilligan's research—and especially her thesis that there is a paradigmatic male ethic of justice and a paradigmatic female ethic of responsibility that qualify as irreducibly different and incommensurable modes of social experience and interpretation—support the main claims of Simmel's essays "Female Culture" and "The Relative and the Absolute in the Problem of the Sexes." See especially Gilligan 1982, chapter 6. Gilligan ties these differences in moral judgment not to biological facts of gender but to differences in the ways the two sexes experience the social world. (See Gilligan 1982, p. 2.) It is in this light that the two ethical paradigms sketched below should be conceived: as two different modes of moral experience or two different ways of constructing a sphere of ethics.

the persons involved, the intentions and motives with which it is linked, and the specific consequences that can be expected to follow from it. The criterion for the resolution of a moral conflict is not the valid application of some general principle but the minimization of harm through the exercise of compassion and care. In the ideal male resolution of a moral conflict, the correct principle is flawlessly applied. In the ideal female resolution, no one gets hurt. In the female ethic, therefore, moral obligations attach primarily to persons and their needs, not to principles and their requirements. The moral imperative of avoiding harm is necessarily tied to the particular psychological, historical, and social conditions of the conflict. This is why the autonomy and generality of the male ethic cannot apply here. The exercise of moral judgment is successful only if it resolves a concrete practical problem of real life, not an abstract hypothetical dilemma. If male justice is formal in the sense that its purpose is the correct application of abstract principles, regardless of the concrete circumstances of the moral situation, then female justice could be called substantive in the sense that its purpose is to exercise compassion and care in specific cases to the end of eliminating harm.

The incommensurability of the male and female modes of moral judgment is guaranteed by the fact that the abstractness and formality of male ethical principles—realized perhaps most fully in the Kantian categorical imperative and in Bentham's utilitarian calculus—detach moral actors from the concrete context of their lives as individuals. This context includes the intentions, motives, and reasons that are linked with their actions and also the historical and social conditions in which their conduct is embedded. As a result, the practical conflict is disengaged from the real sociopsychological background in which moral problems actually arise. This process of abstraction makes an ethic of compassion—or any substantive ethic that focuses upon specific instances of suffering and injustice—impossible. Compassion can be extended to persons only on the basis of a perception of the actual circumstances of their lives: precisely what they have done and suffered, why this has happened, and exactly what it has meant, factors that are excluded from moral consideration by the formal principles of the male ethic. In the female ethic, principles are subordinated to the needs and interests of human life. They stand in the service of personal values and are expected to preserve them. From this standpoint the male ethic, in abstracting morality from the realities of life, sacrifices people to principles and thus legitimizes suffering, oppression, and exploitation insofar as this is required by their strict application.

Given this distinction between an abstract and putatively male ethic of formal justice based on general principles and a contextual and putatively female ethic of substantive justice based on compassion, the exemplar of male justice is Captain Vere in Herman Melville's *Billy Budd, Sailor*. Billy Budd is a young seaman impressed into service on the English warship under Vere's command during the wars with France at the end of the eighteenth century—"Baby" Budd, who knew not immoral intentions, malice, nor even the self-consciousness essential to the loss of moral innocence. In Vere's presence, the evil chief petty officer, Claggart, accuses Billy of plotting mutiny. Under the extreme stress of this accusation, Billy is afflicted by a paralysis of speech. Struck dumb and stuttering, he in effect speaks with his fists, striking Claggart a single lethal blow. To deal with the situation, Vere immediately convenes a drumhead court martial in which his inflexible advocacy of formal justice supercedes conscience, compassion, his own moral intuitions, and any consideration of the concrete complexities of the case.

It is clear that Vere is convinced of Billy's innocence. He knows that Billy intended neither mutiny nor homicide, and he sees the moral ignominy that lies in sentencing such a man to a summary execution. He admits that conscience as well as compassion—the ethic of the heart and "the feminine in man"—call for clemency. Yet he resists all these scruples as irrelevant to the question of Billy's guilt. Although Vere admits that Claggart has been struck dead by an angel of God, still the angel must hang. But why? It is because the question of guilt turns solely on the deed, independent of the factors that motivated it and the circumstances under which it was committed. Under the Mutiny Act, this deed is a capital offense. As an officer with a commission from the Crown, Vere does not conceive himself as a free moral agent. On the contrary, he is an instrument of that law, obliged to execute its requirements without qualification or exception. Thus Vere decides Billy's guilt in a purely formal fashion, detaching his conduct from all considerations that would make it possible to exercise clemency on the basis of conscience or compassion. The act is treated as nothing more than a case that falls under a general principle. Justice consists in the correct, rigorous, and impersonal application of the principle to this case. Vere's obligation, therefore, is not to the person but to the principle. "With mankind," he insists, "forms, measured forms are everything." Billy has violated these forms—albeit unwittingly, unintentionally, and without malice. For all that, he must be sacrificed to the unyielding exigencies of formal justice: "However pitilessly that law may operate in any instances, we nevertheless adhere to it and administer it."

If Melville's Vere is the personification of a formal male justice, perhaps it could be said that the female sense of justice Simmel envisions is personified in Shakespeare's Portia. It is especially illuminating to compare the manner in which Vere resolves the conflict between Billy's subjective moral innocence and the objective requirements of the law with the way Portia resolves the main practical dilemma of *The Merchant of Venice*: the conflict between the Jew's formal legal right to a pound of Antonio's flesh and Antonio's appeal to be protected from a cruel and fatal sentence.

Portia, disguised as a distinguished Roman legal scholar called in by the Duke of Venice to adjudicate the conflict, bases her judgment on the concrete circumstances under which it arose. The bankrupt Bassanio had sought a loan of 3,000 ducats from his friend the merchant Antonio in order to pursue his courtship of Portia. Because all his capital was invested in goods and ships then at sea, Antonio proposed to borrow the money from his enemy, the Jewish usurer Shylock. Antonio despises Jews, he habitually rebukes Shylock as a usurer, and he compromises Shylock's profits by lending money gratis and driving down the rate of interest. The Jew eagerly agrees to lend Antonio the 3,000 ducats for three months on the condition that if he is not repaid by the end of this period, he shall have the right to cut a pound of flesh from any part of Antonio's body he chooses. Antonio, expecting the return of his ships within two months, readily accepts what he somewhat naively regards as an interest-free loan. When the note falls due, he receives word that all his ships have been lost at sea. Thus he must submit to Shylock's contractual right to cut a pound of flesh from his breast. At that point, Antonio, his friends, and even the Duke of Venice himself appeal to the Jew's moral intuitions and conscience and plead with him to act mercifully, confronting him with the enormity of the fine and the fact that Antonio will literally have to repay the loan with his life. In the face of these demands for substantive justice, the Jew becomes the advocate of justice as formal legality. It is not the native Venetians in the drama but only the alien Jew who can legitimately claim that he stands for the law of Venice. Shylock holds that the pound of flesh has been bought and is his by legal right. If this right is denied, it follows that the laws of Venice have no force, in which case all its contracts would be nullified.

Portia's way of handling Shylock's claim is to give him precisely what he asks for: "For as thou urgest justice, be assur'd Thou shalt have justice more than thou desir'st." The Jew is made to forgo his right to a pound of Antonio's flesh, but only by means of a clever manipulation of formal jurisprudence in which Portia manages to beat Shylock, the champion of formal justice, at his own game. The contract with Antonio awards the Jew a pound of flesh if the loan cannot be repaid on time. But it does not give him the right to shed blood. Should he take not only flesh but blood as well, the laws of Venice give the duke the right to confiscate all of Shylock's property. In addition, the contract awards Shylock neither more nor less than a pound of flesh. Should he take either more or less than a pound, even by the smallest of fractions, the law demands the confiscation not only of his goods but of his life as well. Finally, in insisting upon the terms of the contract in spite of the fact that Antonio's friends have offered to repay Shylock three times the amount of the loan, the Jew stands in violation of the law which holds that any alien who threatens the life of a citizen of Venice shall have half his goods awarded to the plaintiff, the other half seized by the state, and his life at the mercy of the duke.

Disguised as a male judge and playing his role, Portia confronts a dilemma of her own: how to satisfy the requirements of female justice in a male world, how to exercise compassion and see that no one gets hurt in a legal system that ignores these substantive considerations and demands the unconditional application of general and impersonal principles that apply to all formally equivalent cases in the same way. The Jew can neither be persuaded nor legally compelled to act compassionately, and compassion cannot be forced in any case: The quality of mercy is not strained. When Bassanio pleads with Portia to subordinate the formal justice of the law to the substantive justice of conscience, to "wrest once the law to your authority," to "do a little wrong" in order to "do a great right," she replies coolly that it must not be. "There is no power in Venice can alter a decree established." In other words, given formal criteria for justice, there is no space for the exercise of compassion. So it seems that Portia's only alternative is to masculinize herself and defeat Shylock on his own chosen ground, achieving what female justice demands, but within the system of male justice and according to its rules. Portia has obviously made a contribution to Venetian justice that exceeds the wits of all the male personae; does it not follow that her performance as judge cannot qualify as an expression of the female character and an objectification of the woman's existence? By playing a male role, does she not fragment her personality, detach her performance from her character, and thus depersonalize her conduct? In other words, it appears that Portia can make a contribution to Venetian legal culture only by entering the male division of labor and objectifying herself according to male criteria.

Two points are relevant here. First, although Portia obviously takes on a male role and even appears disguised as a man, she feminizes this role in such a way that the performance expresses her own values. Thus fragmentation and depersonalization of existence and disengagement of performance from character do not occur here. In addition, the results Portia is able to achieve—even if not all the techniques she employs to reach them—realize her own sense of justice as compassion. Portia's advocacy of justice as the avoidance of harm is the point of her famous speech in which she defends the subordination of formal justice to mercy. She also makes clear her commitment to the view that moral predicates cannot be ascribed to actions in virtue of their abstract qualities but only on the basis of the concrete psychological, historical, and social context in which they are performed. For this reason, it is necessary to examine the intentions and motives of the actor, his relationships to others, and the damage that may fall to the interests of individuals as a result of his action. This is the point of her argument that nothing is good "without respect." Nothing is good in the abstract and independent of the specific circumstances that justify the ascription of goodness to it.

Things become praiseworthy or blameworthy only because of the concrete conditions under which they occur. In settling the conflict, therefore, Portia does not attempt to discover which legal norms are to be impersonally applied in this situation. On the contrary, her aim is to see to it that no one is hurt.[30] Thus she does not weigh claims in an abstract fashion and as instances of the application of general rules, but rather concretely, within the context of actions performed by particular agents against a specific background of intentions, consequences, and interpersonal relations. As a judge, she is a moral agent whose ultimate obligation is to persons rather than to the law. Unlike Vere, she does not regard the law as her ultimate axiom and herself as its instrument. She administers the law not blindly—"legalistically" in the pejorative sense—but rather compassionately, as a tool to minimize the infliction of harm.

It follows that the legal culture personified in Portia's conduct is governed by a prioris that do not hold in the legal system to which Captain Vere is committed. The forms of law do not have the same status, the laws themselves and legal procedures do not have the same purpose, "justice" does not have the same import or meaning, and persons and their conduct are neither conceived nor evaluated in the same way. If there is a distinctively female sense of justice, and if the interests and values of life generate a legal culture anchored in this sense of justice, then it seems that a province of culture fundamentally different from a male legal culture would emerge. This would involve the development of legal norms and rules of procedure that express the female conception of justice. Under this dispensation, the meaning of the concepts of right, responsibility, and obligation would shift accordingly. Suppose it can be said that there is a distinctive female moral language or experience in which minimizing personal damage by exercising care and compassion is the ultimate basis for resolving practical conflicts. In that case, it can also be said that this legal culture could qualify as an objectification of the female mode of being rather than as the masculinization of the

---

30. This includes Shylock. Following Portia's lead, the Duke forfeits his right to demand the Jew's life and commutes the confiscation of one-half his goods to a mere fine. Antonio also forgoes his right to half of Shylock's property and even proposes that the fine be quashed if the Jew will agree to certain conditions.

woman which occurs when she submits to the a prioris of a male culture. In other words, these considerations suggest that there is no obstacle in principle to the feminization of culture, in the sense that specific cultural forms could indeed qualify as objectifications of the woman's experience.

On the other hand, these considerations do not respond to what is perhaps the fundamental implicit question posed by Simmel's writings on women and culture, the problem of a feminist politics of culture. Could there be a female culture—an ensemble of feminized cultural forms—in which objectification does not generate the processes of reification and instrumentalization that are responsible for the fragmentation and disintegration of personal culture? In view of Simmel's concept of modern culture, it seems that the basic political problem of modernity—the conditions for a mode of cultural objectification that does not become self-destructive—has no solution. If that is the case, then this problem would presumably be recalcitrant to a feminist politics of culture as well. Recall that modern culture is defined by two processes: the proliferation of cultural forms, which become increasingly independent of one another and remote from the interests and values of the persons who are subject to them; and the increasing internal complexity of each form, as a result of which the realization of authentic cultural values requires an indefinitely long chain of purely instrumental values. A highly differentiated division of labor that depends upon the specialization of the cultural actor and the depersonalization of his activity is both an essential condition and an inevitable concomitant of these two developments. If reification and instrumentalization are the constitutive processes of modernity, it seems to follow that there is only one way in which a feminist politics of culture could solve the basic political problem of modern culture: by demodernizing it, by reducing both the proliferation of cultural forms and the internal complexity of each form, thereby limiting the level of the division of labor as well. Of course this is possible only if the feminization of culture could counter the force of these interlinked factors which threaten the identity of the individual and the coherence of his personal culture. Feminization would thereby qualify as demodernization. This seems to be the only possibility for a female culture in which objectification will not terminate in cultural anomie by destroying the conditions for the possibility of subjective culture.

The obvious empirical question is, of course, whether this hypothetical possibility is not purely utopian, an interesting speculative vision that cannot be realized for historical and sociological reasons. This is an immensely complicated question, which clearly cannot be resolved here. Consider, for example, the thesis that the definitive properties of modern culture are tied in the final analysis to demographic phenomena: unprecedentedly and increasingly large numbers of persons and their artifacts. If this is the case, is it empirically possible to reduce the variety and complexity of cultural forms when the population of cities runs to tens of millions and that of nation states to hundreds of millions, when the masses have been thoroughly politicized and the economy irreversibly internationalized? To put this in another way, is there perhaps an elective affinity between the quantitative facts of modern society and the complexity of modern culture? If the persistence of large formal organizations in every domain of modern life is our fate because we are in the grip of large numbers, does it not follow that the proliferation and internal differentiation of cultural forms must also be our fate for the same reason? If so, then the increasing and irreversible objectification of modern culture is an ultimate datum, a brute fact of history, and not a problem that is accessible to any politics of culture, including an ensemble of cultural forms that expresses the interests and values of a characteristically female mode of experience.

THE ESSAYS

Among his contemporaries, Simmel passed as a dazzling stylist and a brilliantly original writer. Regardless of how this judgment is assessed today, the reader who is not familiar with Simmel's style may be in for some surprises. In any given essay, Simmel is likely to be concerned with a considerable range of issues that are not clearly differentiated and may not even be explicitly identified. In a single text in which he discusses the division of labor, female sexuality, beauty, poetry and drama as male art forms, and the bourgeois household, several quite different kinds of problem—sociological, ethical, aesthetic, epistemological, and metaphysical—may be raised. However, he may provide no clear indication, perhaps not even a hint or an intimation, of the movement from one kind of problem to another. As a result, the reader may easily get the impression that the dynamic of the inquiry itself is more important to Simmel than its clarity and a careful defense of the conclusions that are reached. There also seems to be a sense in which he regards style as more significant than substance. On this view, Simmel qualifies as a virtuoso intellectual performer, adept at creating astonishing literary pyrotechnics. However, it is not clear that he has any contribution to make to systematic scientific research. Simmel's essays— including the ones presented here—typically exhibit an anecdotal, fragmented, and inconsequential quality. This can easily lead the reader to conclude that Simmel is an intellectual coquette, engaged in a high form of literary play which is primarily intended not to instruct or enlighten but to exercise that seductive charm and fascination he describes in the essay on flirtation.

Consider also Simmel's usual method of approaching a theme by means of oblique suggestions and allusions. The major points appear in a setting of ingenious and sometimes brilliant insights. However, they remain fugitive and undeveloped. Eschewing a systematic analysis of problems and a detailed development of arguments, Simmel seems to move swiftly, effortlessly, and often unexpectedly from one theme to another. In addition, his work does not exhibit the conventional scholarly apparatus of footnotes, bibliographical citations, and references to the contemporary literature. Is it conceivable that Kant scholarship could be written without footnotes or references? This is what Simmel managed to achieve in his book on Kant (Simmel 1921). In addition, he rarely refers to the work of any living scholar and never cites the writings of his German contemporaries who were also working on the problems of his research. Although it is obvious that Simmel was powerfully influenced by Dilthey's investigations into the foundations of the sociocultural sciences, neither Dilthey's name nor a single reference to any of his writings ever appears in Simmel's publications. This strongly suggests either ignorance and naiveté—impossible in the case of Simmel—or arrogance and conceit.

In the light of these considerations, it would not be an exaggeration to represent Simmel's work as a persistent and self-conscious attempt to resist a major conclusion of the arguments that Max Weber develops in the lecture "Science as a Vocation" (Weber, 1958). Weber claims that the professionalization of intellectual life is an inevitable consequence of the distinctive rationalization of modern Western culture. The alienation of the wage laborer is merely one instance of a much more comprehensive process that embraces the intellectual as well. Both lose the ability to control the instruments of production and exchange that are essential to their activity: in the case of the intellectual, libraries, institutes, archives, and funds, the increasingly complex and extensive apparatus on which modern research depends. Because of the irresistible intensification of the division of labor, it is inevitable that intellectual work also becomes increasingly specialized. Modern science and scholarship are bureaucratized. In the modern era, only naiveté or self-deception can continue to sustain a belief in the pursuit of knowledge as the path to true being, God, art, or happiness. The intellectual who is faithful to his calling and attempts to satisfy the demands of the day does not pursue the life of the mind in order to express his personality or advocate a weltanschauung. On the contrary, the differentiation of intellectual labor requires that he sacrifice both his personality and his metaphysical commitments to the specialized requirements of a professional discipline. According to Weber, modern science is "chained to the course of progress." Like the technological apparatus of industrial civilization, it functions in a quasi-mechanical fashion and according to principles that render individual accomplishments relatively ephemeral and insignificant. Like the iron cage of capitalism in which human needs are sacrificed to the exigencies of production, there is a sense in which science in the modern world has also become the prison house of the mind: Within the domain of institutionalized science and academic scholarship, creativity and innovation must be accommodated to the specialized criteria of achievement that govern the various professional disciplines. The attempt to resist these criteria may be based on a variety of motives, ranging from moral integrity and metaphysical consistency to opportunism and sensationalism. However, any such attempt is invariably tantamount to a declaration of independence from the pursuit of science itself. It is an admission—whether explicit and self-conscious or covert and unwitting—that the intellectual's enterprise lies beyond the legitimate limits of scientific inquiry. It follows that the thinker who refuses to submit to the specialized demands of a scientific or scholarly profession marks himself as a scientific pariah.

Simmel's work is committed to the rejection of the methodological asceticism and metaphysical pessimism of Weber's conception of modern science and scholarship. Throughout his career, Simmel explored a vast range of questions and pursued an immense variety of research interests. From the perspective of the conventional academic intellectual, Simmel's problems are likely to appear hopelessly misconceived and impossibly recalcitrant, and the scope of his work must seem extremely suspicious, perhaps even somewhat shocking: sociological theory; sociological studies of various aspects of modernity, including money, freedom, individuality, the city, the stranger, the role of numbers in modern life, and the intellectualization of life; Kant scholarship; comparative studies of Goethe, Kant, Schopenhauer, and Nietzsche; an aesthetic and philosophical study of Rembrandt; studies on metaphysics and what would today be called metaphilosophy; and many essays on an improbable and apparently incoherent collection of subjects—love, death, fate, meals, tact, women, the actor, sexuality, Rodin, Bergson, flirtation, Stefan George, and the personality of God, to mention only a few. Anyone who undertakes all this obviously invites the objection that his aims are absurdly ambitious. And any academic intellectual who writes essays on Venice, the Alps, autumn on the Rhine, Goethe and women, the philosophy of landscape, and roses, just as obviously opens himself to charges of frivolity and intellectual coquetry.

All these qualities of the Simmelian intellectual style—the dazzling but perplexing mode of thought, the disposition to investigate quite different problems more or less simultaneously and without any clear indication of how they are linked, the inclination to eschew careful analysis and detailed argument in favor of pregnant examples and glittering insights, and the playful and inconclusive quality of the inquiry itself, in which aesthetic considerations frequently seem to outweigh the requirements of science—are fully in evidence in the essays that follow.[31]

31. Max Weber's incomplete critique of Simmel's work covers some of these same points. As a trenchant analysis of Simmel's intellectual style, it has been surpassed only by Lukács's appreciation, written shortly after Simmel's death. See Weber (1972) and Lukács (1958). The inconclusive and essayistic quality of Simmel's thought is discussed in considerable detail in Frisby (1981). It is linked to Frisby's conception of Simmel's "perspectivism": the view that there is no fixed standpoint on the basis of which reality can be constituted, a position that, in Frisby's view, seems to end in "a thorough-going relativism" (Frisby 1981, p. 155).

REFERENCES

Adorno, Theodor W.
1965   "Henkel, Krug und frühe Erfahrung." Pp. 9–20 in Siegfried Unseld (ed.), *Ernst Bloch zu ehren*. Frankfurt: Suhrkamp.

Bebel, August
1971   *Women under Socialism* (trans. by Daniel de Leon). New York: Schocken.

Broch, Hermann
1947   *The Sleepwalkers, A Trilogy* (trans. by Willa and Edwin Muir). New York: Pantheon.

Burstyn, Joan N.
1980   *Victorian Education and the Ideal of Womanhood*. Totowa, N.J.: Barnes and Noble Books.

Eisenstein, Zillah R.
1981   *The Radical Future of Liberal Feminism*. New York: Longman.

Eisenstein, Zillah R. (ed.)
1979   *Capitalist Patriarchy and the Case for Socialist Feminism*. New York: Monthly Review Press.

Evans, Richard J.
1976   *The Feminist Movement in Germany, 1894–1933*. London and Beverly Hills: Sage Publications.

Frisby, David
1981   *Sociological Impressionism: A Reassessment of Georg Simmel's Social Theory*. London: Heinemann.

Gilligan, Carol
1977   "In a Different Voice: Women's Conceptions of Self and Morality." *Harvard Educational Review* 47, pp. 52–88.

1982   *In a Different Voice: Psychological Theory and Women's Development*. Cambridge, Mass.: Harvard University Press.

Hackett, Amy
1976a   "The Politics of Feminism in Wilhelmine Germany, 1890–1918." Ph.D. dissertation, Columbia University.

1976b   "Feminism and Liberalism in Wilhelmine Germany." Pp. 127–36 in Berenice A. Carroll (ed.), *Liberating Women's History*. Urbana: University of Illinois Press.

Harrison, Brian
1978   *Separate Spheres: The Opposition to Women's Suffrage in Britain*. New York: Holmes and Meier.

Kaplan, Marion A.
1977   "German-Jewish Feminism: The Jüdischer Frauenbund, 1904–
1938." Ph.D. dissertation, Columbia University.

1979   *The Jewish Feminist Movement in Germany: The Campaign of
the Jüdischer Frauenbund, 1904–1938*. Westport, Conn.: Greenwood
Press.

Lawrence, P. A. (ed.)
1976   *Georg Simmel: Sociologist and European*. New York: Barnes and
Nobel Books.

Lieber, Hans-Joachim
1974   *Kulturkritik und Lebensphilosophie*. Darmstadt: Wissenschaft-
liche Buchgesellschaft.

Lieber, Hans-Joachim, and Peter Furth
1958   "Zur Dialektik der Simmelschen Konzeption einer formalen Soziologie." Pp. 39–59 in Kurt Gassen and Michael Landmann (eds.), *Buch des
Dankes an Georg Simmel*. Berlin: Duncker and Humblot.

Lukács, Georg
1958   "Georg Simmel." Pp. 171–76 in Kurt Gassen and Michael Landmann (eds.), *Buch des Dankes an Georg Simmel*. Berlin: Duncker and
Humblot.

1971   *History and Class Consciousness* (trans. by Rodney Livingstone).
Cambridge, Mass.: MIT Press.

1981   *The Destruction of Reason* (trans. by Peter Palmer). Atlantic High-
lands, N.J.: Humanities Press.

McMillan, James F.
1981   *Housewife or Harlot: The Place of Women in French Society,
1870–1940*. New York: St. Martin's.

Mann, Thomas
1961   *Buddenbrooks*. (trans. by H. T. Lowe-Porter). New York: Ran-
dom House.

Melville, Herman
1962   *Billy Budd, Sailor*. Chicago: University of Chicago Press.

Mitchell, Juliet
1971   *Women's Estate*. New York: Pantheon.

1974   *Psychoanalysis and Feminism*. New York: Pantheon.

Oldenburg, Henry
1965–69   *Correspondence*, 6 volumes (ed. by A. R. Hall and Marie Boas
Hall). Madison: University of Wisconsin Press.

Quataert, J. H.
1979 *Reluctant Feminists in German Social Democracy, 1885–1917.*
Princeton: Princeton University Press.

Rosenberg, Rosalind
1982 *Beyond Separate Spheres: Intellectual Roots of Modern Feminism.* New Haven: Yale University Press.

Rossi, Alice S. (ed.)
1970 *Essays on Sex Equality. John Stuart Mill and Harriet Taylor Mill.*
Chicago: University of Chicago Press.

Rowbotham, Sheila
1972 *Women, Resistance, and Revolution.* New York: Pantheon.

1973 *Woman's Consciousness, Man's World.* Baltimore: Penguin.

Simmel, Georg
1906 *Kant und Goethe: Zur Geschichte der modernen Weltanschauung.*
Berlin: Marquardt.

1910 *Hauptprobleme der Philosophie.* Leipzig: Göschen.

1913 *Goethe.* Leipzig: Klinkhardt and Biermann.

1919 *Rembrandt: Ein kunstphilosophischer Versuch.* 2nd edition. Leipzig: Kurt Wolff.

1921 *Kant. Sechzehn Vorlesungen gehalten an der Berliner Universität.*
5th edition. Munich and Leipzig: Duncker and Humblot.

1922a *Lebensanschauung, Vier Metaphysische Kapitel.* 2nd edition.
Munich and Leipzig: Duncker and Humblot.

1922b *Zur Philosophie der Kunst.* Potsdam: Kiepenheuer.

1923a *Philosophische Kultur: Gesammelte Essais.* 3rd edition. Potsdam:
Kiepenheuer.

1923b *Schopenhauer und Nietzsche: Ein Vortragszyklus.* 3rd. edition.
Munich and Leipzig: Duncker and Humblot.

1957 *Brücke und Tür* (ed. by Michael Landmann). Stuttgart: K. F.
Koehler.

1964 *Einleitung in die Moralwissenschaft: Eine Kritik der ethischen
Grundbegriffe.* Volume 1. 4th edition. Aalen: Scienta Verlag (a reprint of
the 1892–93 edition, Berlin: Hertz).

1967 *Fragmente und Aufsätze aus dem Nachlass und Veröffentlichungen der letzten Jahre* (ed. by Gertrud Kantorowicz). Hildesheim:
Georg Olms.

1977 *The Problems of the Philosophy of History* (trans. by Guy Oakes).
New York: The Free Press.

1978 *The Philosophy of Money* (trans. by Tom Bottomore and David Frisby). London: Routledge and Kegan Paul.

1980 *Essays on Interpretation in Social Science* (trans. by Guy Oakes). Totowa, N.J.: Rowman and Littlefield.

Smith, Bonnie G.

1981 *Ladies of the Leisure Class: The Bourgeoises of Northern France in the Nineteenth Century.* Princeton: Princeton University Press.

Thönnessen, Werner

1973 *The Emancipation of Women: The Rise and Decline of the Women's Movement in German Social Democracy, 1863–1933* (trans. by Joris de Bres). London: Pluto Press.

Troeltsch, Ernst

1922 *Der Historismus und seine Probleme.* Tübingen: J. C. B. Mohr.

Unger, Roberto Mangabeira

1975 *Knowledge and Politics.* New York: The Free Press.

Weber, Max

1958 *From Max Weber: Essays in Sociology* (trans., ed., and with an introduction by H. H. Gerth and C. Wright Mills). New York: Oxford University Press.

1972 "Georg Simmel as Sociologist" (trans. by Donald N. Levine). *Social Research* 39: 155–63.

Wolff, Kurt H. (ed.)

1959 *Georg Simmel, 1858–1918.* Columbus: Ohio State University Press.

THE ESSAYS

FEMALE CULTURE

Culture can be regarded as the perfection of individuals achieved as a result of the objectified spirit at work in the history of the species. Subjective being appears as cultured in its unity and totality by virtue of the fact that it is consummated in the acquisition of objective values: the values of morality and knowledge, art and religion, social formations and the expressive forms of the inner life. Thus culture is a distinctive synthesis of the subjective and the objective spirit. Its ultimate purpose, of course, can lie only in the enrichment of individuals. However, the contents of the objective spirit must first be juxtaposed to this process of perfection as autonomous and detached, both from those who create the contents and from those who appropriate them. Only by this means can they then be incorporated into the process as its instruments or stages. As a result, these contents—all that is expressed and formed, what exists ideally and what has real force, the complex of which constitutes the cultural capital of an era—may be designated as its "objective culture." From the determination of this objective culture, we can distinguish the following as the problem of "subjective culture": To what degree, both extensively and intensively, do individuals have a share in the contents of objective culture?

From the perspective of both reality and value, these two concepts are quite independent of each other. The great mass of personalities that comes into question may be excluded from a highly developed objective culture. On the other hand, this same mass can participate in a relatively primitive culture in such a way that subjective culture attains a relatively extraordinary level. Value judgments vary in a corresponding fashion. Those who have purely individualist convictions, and especially those who have purely social convictions, will link the entire significance of culture to the question of how many persons participate in it and to what extent. How much cultivation and happiness, beauty and morality, does the life realized in the individual draw from it? On the other hand, consider those who have a commitment not only to the utility of things but also to the things themselves, not merely to the turbulent stream of action, pleasure, and suffering but also to the timeless meaning of the forms on which the spirit has left its stamp. They will be interested only in the development of objective culture. They will appeal to the consideration that the objective value of a work of art, a piece of knowledge, a religious idea, or even a law or an ethical norm is quite irrelevant to the question of how frequently or infrequently the fortuitous course of the reality of life has incorporated all this into itself.

The two value questions posed by the modern women's movement also divide at the point that these two tendencies branch off. The genesis of this movement seemed to confine it completely to the course of subjective culture. Insofar as women proposed to move into the forms of life and achievements of men, for them the question concerned their personal participation in cultural goods that already existed and to which they had merely been denied access, regardless of whether these goods might provide them with a new source of happiness, new obligations, or a new form of personality. In this case, the struggle is invariably only on behalf of individual persons, regardless of how many millions of people may have a stake in it in both the present and the future. It is not a struggle for something that in itself transcends everything individual and personal. How often a value is realized is at issue here, not the creation of objectively new values. Perhaps all the eudaemonistic, ethical, and social emphases of the women's movement are grounded in this tendency. However, the other tendency, which is much more abstract and produced by a need that is much less pressing, does not disappear: the question of whether qualitatively new entities and an expansion of the objective content of culture arise from this movement, the question not only of a multiplication or reproduction of what already exists but rather of creation as well.

Suppose that the women's movement, in accordance with the view of its advocates, immeasurably extends the domain of subjective culture. Or suppose, as its opponents prophesy, that it threatens to debase the value of subjective culture. The gains the women's movement produces for the contents of objective culture would be independent of both cases. The prospects for the latter development will be considered here. More precisely, we shall consider the *basis* for these prospects: the fundamental relations of the female nature to objective culture.

In this context, it is important at the outset to affirm the fact that human culture, even as regards its purely objective contents, is not asexual. As a result of its objectivity, there is no sense in which culture exists in a domain that lies beyond men and women. It is rather the case that, with the exception of a very few areas, our objective culture is thoroughly male. It is men who have created art and industry, science and commerce, the state and religion. The belief that there is a purely "human" culture for which the difference between man and woman is irrelevant has its origin in the same premise from which it follows that such a culture does not exist—the naive identification of the "human" with "man." Many languages even use the same word for both concepts.

At this point, I shall not consider the issue of whether this masculine character of the objective elements of our culture is a result of the inner nature of the sexes or is a consequence of male dominance, a matter that really has no relation to the question of culture. In any case, this naive identification is responsible for the fact that deficient performances in the most diverse areas are degraded as "feminine" while outstanding performances of women are celebrated as "thoroughly manly." It is why not only the scope but also the nature of our cultural activity turn on specifically male energies and emotions and a distinctively male intellectuality.

This is important for culture as a whole, and especially for those strata that can be called semiproductive. These are the strata in which nothing absolutely new is brought forth from the spiritual springs of creativity. However, they are also not characterized by mechanical reproduction according to models that are exactly prescribed. On the contrary, these strata constitute a certain middle ground. Thus far, cultural history has not adequately investigated this distinctive quality, which is of infinite importance for the more subtle aspects of the structure of society. In many areas of technology and commerce, science and warfare, literary activity and art, innumerable achievements of what could be called secondary originality are called for: achievements which take place within given forms and on the basis of given presuppositions, but which also demonstrate initiative, distinctiveness, and creative power. The claims of the specifically male energies are especially evident in these cases. That is because the forms and presuppositions in question have their origin in the male spirit. They transmit its character to these achievements, which might be described as epigonal.

I shall single out only one example of this masculine nature of cultural contents that seem to be completely neutral. Frequently the "legal antipathy" of women is stressed: their opposition to legal norms and judgments. However there is no sense in which this necessarily implies an animus against the law itself; instead, it is only against *male* law, which is the only law we have, and for this reason seems to us to be the law as such. In the same way, our historically defined morality, individualized by considerations of both time and place, seems to us to fulfill the conditions of the concept of morality in general. The female "sense of justice," which differs from the male in many respects, would create a different law as well. The entire logical problematic of this sense should not conceal the fact that, ultimately, legislation as well as the administration of justice rest on a basis that can be characterized only in this way. Suppose that there were an objectively determinable ultimate purpose of all law. In that case, of course, it would be possible to construe every single legal definition on its basis and in a way that is, in principle, purely rational. However, this ultimate purpose itself could be posited only by a metalogical act that would constitute nothing more than another form of this "sense of justice" and its crystallization in a stable and distinctive logical entity. But since this has not happened, the sense of justice remains in a more or less fluid state, in which it effectively and decisively enters into every single definition and decision, just as some quantum of the undifferentiated protoplasm still remains in almost every cell of even the fully developed animal organism. Thus every immanently defined and pervasive sense of justice would produce its own law. A body of law that developed in this fashion on the basis of the specifically female sense of justice could be denied acknowledgment as an objectively valid body of "law" only because the objective is a priori identified with the male.

However, the fact that the real contents of our culture exhibit a male character, rather than their apparently neutral character, is grounded in a multifaceted interweaving of historical and psychological motives. Culture, which in the final analysis is a state of subjects or persons, does not trace its path merely through objectivations of the spirit. On the contrary, with the progress of each of its great periods, this sphere of real objects becomes increasingly extensive. The sojourn of individuals—with their interests, development, and productivity—becomes increasingly protracted in this transitional region. Ultimately, objective culture takes on the appearance of culture as such. Its consummation in subjects no longer seems to be the aim and purpose of culture but rather the purely private concern of these subjects, and otherwise is of no real relevance. The accelerated rate of development applies more to things than to persons. The "separation of the worker from the instruments of production" appears as only a quite specific economic instance of a general tendency to shift the praxiological and axiological emphasis of culture away from human beings and onto the perfection and self-sufficient development of objects.

This objectification of our culture, which requires no proof, stands in a most intimate mutual relationship with its other most salient characteristic: its specialization. Suppose that the person, instead of constituting a whole, increasingly becomes nothing more than a dependent and inherently insignificant aspect of such a whole. In that case, it becomes increasingly difficult for him either to bring to bear the unified totality of his personality on his work or to recognize this totality in his work. There is an invariable connection between the inherent uniformity of the performance and that of the performer. It is exhibited most significantly in a work of art, the distinctive and self-sufficient unity of which requires a homogeneous creator and unconditionally resists all fabrication on the basis of differentiated and specialized performances. If these specialized performances are present, the subject as such is detached from them. The product of labor is coordinated with an impersonal structure whose objective requirements it is obliged to meet. This product is juxtaposed to each of those who contributed to it, as a totality which he does not comprehend and which does not reflect his self. If the objective element of our culture did not occupy such a decisive prerogative over its personal element, then the modern division of labor simply would not be feasible. And conversely, if this division of labor did not exist, then the contents of our culture could not have that objectivistic character.

However, as the entire history of work demonstrates, it is obvious that the division of labor is incomparably more congruent with the male nature than with the female. Even today, when it is precisely the division of labor that has removed from the household a large number of differentiated tasks that were formerly carried out within its unity, the activity of the housewife is more diversified and less specialized than any male occupation. It seems as if the man has more opportunity to allow his energy to flow in a unilinear direction without threatening his personality. This is precisely because he experiences this differentiated activity from a purely objective standpoint, and as detached from his own subjective life, a standpoint clearly distinguished from what could be called the private existence of his subjective life. Moreover—and this is quite curious and difficult to express conceptually—this holds true even if he is committed to this objective and specialized task with a total intensity.

However—and this is the second point—the more refined sensitivity and the pronounced vulnerability of women may also rest on this disposition rather than upon the more fragile or delicate structure of their individual psychic elements. There is a sense in which the lack of differentiation and the self-contained uniformity of woman's psychic nature make it impossible for any attack upon her to remain localized. Every assault continues from the point of attack until it covers the entire personality, in which case it quite readily affects all possible points that are easily vulnerable or injured. It is repeatedly said of women that they are more easily offended than men under the same circumstances. However, this simply means that they frequently perceive a singular attack aimed at some specific point as touching their entire person. This is because they have a more integral nature, in which the part has not differentiated itself from the whole and taken on an autonomous life.

This fundamental structure of the female nature—which achieves historical expression only in its estrangement from culture as specialized and objective—can be epitomized in a psychological trait: fidelity. Fidelity signifies that the totality and integrity of the psyche are indissolubly connected with one single element of its contents. There is probably universal agreement concerning the observed fact that women, compared with men, have a more constant nature. This begins with the woman's dependence upon old articles of possession—her own as well as those belonging to persons dear to her—and also upon "recollections," tangible as well as those of the most intimate sort. The undivided unity of her nature holds together whatever has taken place. As regards values and feelings that were once associated with each thing and related to the same center, the unity of her nature links these values and feelings to the thing in question in such a way that they are very difficult to separate.

The male is less pious. This is due to his differentiated quality, as a result of which he sees things more in terms of their autonomous objectivity. Consider the capacity to decompose oneself into a plurality of distinctly different essential tendencies, to detach the periphery from the center, and to make interests and activities independent of their integral interconnection. All this creates a disposition in favor of infidelity. In this case, the development can seize upon first one and then another interest, bring the person into changing forms, and make each present moment completely free to choose on its own terms and in a purely objective fashion. However, this presents the development with a profusion of different modes of action, each of which has the same unprejudiced status—a possibility that fidelity excludes.

From the perspective of the logic of psychology, differentiation and objectivity are the antitheses of fidelity. Fidelity unconditionally fuses the totality of the personality with a single interest, feeling, and experience. Simply because such an interest, feeling, and experience existed, fidelity remains fused with them. For this reason, it represents an obstacle to that retreat of the ego from its individual embodiments. There is something faithless in the separation of the person from the object. In this respect, it is opposed to the more constant nature of women. It estranges women—inwardly, of course—from a productive culture that is objectified on the basis of its specialization, and specialized on the basis of its objectivity.

Thus, insofar as women are lacking in objective cultural accomplishments, this need not signify a dynamic deficiency in relation to a general human requirement. On the contrary, it may signify only the incongruity between a mode of being in which all the contents of life exist solely through the energy of an indivisible subjective center with which they are directly fused, and authentication in a world of objects as structured by the differentiated nature of the male.

It is true that men are more objective than women. However, suppose that the male is regarded quite self-evidently as the more consummate being, and that a life in which there is no differentiation of the individual from the totality is regarded as deficient and "undeveloped." This is possible only by means of a vicious circle. From the outset, the relative value of the male and the female is decided on the basis of a male rather than a neutral value idea. It follows that only a thoroughly radical dualism can help us here. The naive conflation of male values with values as such can give way only if the female existence as such is acknowledged as having a basis fundamentally different from the male and a stream of life flowing in a fundamentally different direction: two existential totalities, each structured according to a completely autonomous rule.

This naive conflation is based on historical power relationships that are logically expressed in the fateful dual meaning of the concept of the "objective." On the one hand, the objective seems to be a purely neutral idea, equidistant above the one-sidedness of both the male and the female. On the other hand, the objective is also the specific form of achievement that corresponds to the distinctively male mode of being. The former is a conception of transhistorical and transpsychological abstraction. The latter is a historical configuration that has its origins in the differential quality of masculinity. As a result, the criteria that are derived from the latter conception employ the same word and assume the same thoroughly ideal status characteristic of the former conception. Thus the being whose nature excludes the possibility of authentication by means of the specifically male conception of objectivity seems to be devalued from the standpoint of the transhistorical and inherently human conception of objectivity (which in our culture is either not realized at all or is realized only very sporadically).

This male capacity for not allowing his personal existence to be torn apart by a specialized performance that entails no inherent psychic unity is due to the fact that he places this performance in the remote distance of objectivity. It seems that this is exactly what the female nature lacks, not in the sense of a gap, but rather in that what is expressed here as a deficiency stems completely from the positive qualities of this nature. For if there is any sense in which the distinctive psychic quality of woman's nature can be expressed symbolically, it is this: Its periphery is more closely connected with its center and its aspects are more completely integrated into the whole than holds true for the male nature. Here the authentication of the single individual does not lie in a distinctive development and a differentiation from the self with its emotive and affective centers; a process shifts the performance into the domain of the objective, with the result that its lifeless specialization becomes compatible with a complete and animated personal existence (which, of course, does not deny that there are male phenomena in which the latter suffers at the expense of the former).

At this point, I shall consider only two aspects of this homogeneity of the female nature. They are specific and quite remote from one another. Perhaps we designate them with concepts that are as negative as diffuseness and lack of objectivity only because, in the main, language and concept formation conform to the male nature.

As regards the introduction of female prison attendants, experienced penitentiary experts have stressed that only quite well-educated women should be accepted. As a rule, the male prisoner is quite docile in obeying his guard, even if the guard is far beneath him in education and culture. However, female prisoners have almost always created difficulties for a female guard inferior to them in education and culture. In other words, the man differentiates his total personality from the individual relationship in which he finds himself. He experiences this relationship in a purely objective fashion, detached from all factors that are external to it. The woman, on the other hand, cannot permit this momentary relationship to transpire in an impersonal fashion. On the contrary, she experiences it as inseparable from her integral total being. For this reason, she draws the consequences and makes the comparisons which the relationship between her complete personality and that of her female guard implies.

The opposition at stake here spans the relationship between the completely general nature of women and the completely general form of our culture. Thus, within this culture, the female performance will be all the more inhibited the more this most universal and formal element confronts her as a *demand*. This holds true most certainly in the case of original creativity. If contents which are already formed are taken up and their combinations are further worked out, this rather easily results in an accommodation to the total character of the area of culture in question. However, if a spontaneous creation emerges from the most distinctive qualities of the subject, this requires an absolutely active and total formation, beginning with the most elemental features of the contents at stake. In the extreme case, this activity finds no aspect of the general form in the material itself. On the contrary, the distance from the material to the general form must be surmounted step by step and without any residue by the creative psyche. This results in the sequence in which female activities are successful within an objective culture defined in male terms.

Within the arts, the woman's domain lies in those which are reproductive: from the art of dramatic acting (to be discussed below from another aspect) and musical performance, to that most distinctive type of embroidery in which the mark of incomparable skill and industry consists precisely in its reproduction of a "given" pattern. In the sciences, her abilities as a collector and a "carrier" are noteworthy; and this capacity to work with what she is given progressively advances to her considerable accomplishments as a teacher— for, all its functional independence notwithstanding, teaching still consists in transmitting what is given. In short, within the limits of hitherto existing culture, woman is more successful to the extent that the material of her work has already incorporated the spirit of this culture—that is, the male spirit—into itself. She fails to the extent that an act of original production is demanded: in other words, an act which requires that she commit her original energies, which are a priori quite differently disposed, solely to the forms that are required by the objective—and thus, the male—culture.

It could be said, however, that there is a twofold sense in which this culture is male. It is male not only because it transpires in an objective form determined by the division of labor but also because the realizations of this form prescribe single accomplishments and synthesize the elements of these accomplishments into specific professions in a way that conforms to the distinctive rhythm and intention of the male capacity. Thus, independent of the fundamental difficulty concerning forms noted above, there would still be an inadequacy, and even a disavowal, of the creation of new intensities and qualities of culture if women undertook to become natural scientists or engineers, physicians or artists, in the same sense that men are.

Of course this will happen often enough, and the quantum of subjective culture will still be amply increased. However, if objective culture is to exist, and if women are to accommodate themselves to its form, then new nuances and a new extension of its limits are to be expected from women only if they accomplish something that *men cannot do*. This is the core of the entire problem, the pivotal point of the relationship between the women's movement and objective culture. In certain areas, a decomposition of the activity that is now regarded as an objective unity (even though, in reality, this synthesis of partial functions conformed to the male mode of work) will create distinctively female spheres of activity. English workers have carried this principle out in a limited area of material life. There are many cases in which women have used their inferior and cheaper standard of living in order to undercut men. As a result, the standard wage declines, so that in general the trade unions are most bitterly opposed to the use of female labor in industry. Some trade unions— the cotton weavers and the stocking weavers, for example—have found a way out of this problem by introducing a standard list of wages for all factory work, even for the most trivial constituent functions. Everyone receives the same pay for these functions, regardless of whether they are performed by men or women.

This was intended as a way of eliminating competition between men and women. However, it has developed, as if independently, a division of labor in which women in a sense have monopolized the functions for which their physical powers and skills are adequate, leaving to men those functions that conform to *their* abilities. The best expert on conditions among English industrial workers offers the following judgment: "As regards manual labor, the women form a special class of workers who have abilities and needs that differ from those of the men. In order to maintain both sexes in the same state of health and performance capability, a *differentiation of tasks* is frequently necessary." Here, therefore, there is a sense in which the immense problem of female cultural activity is already solved in a naive fashion. The new line is drawn through the complex of tasks, connecting those points for which distinctively female abilities have a predisposition and defining them as special occupations. Even in this context, it holds true that women do something that men are unable to do. Although they were previously done by men, the tasks that conform to the powers of women are certainly better performed by distinctively female labor.

I shall not consider this possibility in any further detail. Even for *knowledge*, it may become apparent only in the domain of praxis. At this point, I shall turn to the other possibility: that there is a sense in which a performance that is both more original and more specifically female develops in the spaces left by the male performance. Even in the domain of science, only quite sporadic observations are possible in this context, perhaps chiefly in the case of medicine. Here the question does not concern the—certainly very considerable—practical and social value of the female physician, who has the same abilities and does the same work as the male. On the contrary, the issue is whether we can expect from the female physician the sort of qualitative advance of medical culture that cannot be attained by male techniques. It seems to me that this is indeed the case. This is because, to no small degree, both diagnosis and therapy depend upon the ability to empathize with the condition of the patient. Objective and clinical methods of examination often come to a premature conclusion unless they are supplemented by a subjective knowledge of the condition and feelings of the patient that is either direct and instinctive or is mediated by what the patient says. I regard this sort of knowledge as a universally operative a priori of the medical art. We tend to be unaware of it only because it is self-evident. This is, of course, why its gradations, with their remarkably nuanced conditions and consequences, have not yet been investigated.

However, these are conditions that must always obtain to *some* degree. The extent to which they are satisfied determines the limits of the physician's understanding. They include a certain constitutional analogy between the physician and the patient: the characteristically obscure but in this regard no less certain and decisive fact that the inner recreation of the state of the patient is undoubtedly based on and determined in its extent by the consideration that the physician is also a being of the same kind. It is in this sense that a neurologist of considerable experience once claimed that a thorough medical diagnosis of certain nervous states is possible only if the physician has experienced similar states.

The conclusion therefore follows that, in relation to women, the female physician will frequently produce the more accurate diagnosis and have the more subtly refined sense for the correct treatment of the individual case. In the domain of pure science, she should also be able to discover typical connections that are indetectable by the man. Thus she would make distinctive contributions to *objective* culture. This is because, in possessing the same constitution as the patient, the woman has a tool of knowledge that is denied the man. I am inclined to think that the fact that the woman is less constrained vis-à-vis the female physician not only is due to the obvious motives, but also stems from the feeling that in many respects she is better understood by a woman than by a man. This holds true especially for women of the lower classes. Since their means of expression are deficient, they must depend more upon being understood in an instinctive fashion. Thus in this case as well, there could be a purely scientific sense in which women, *because of their sex*, could accomplish something that is not possible for men.

On the basis of the same assumption—that a different form of knowledge is based on a different mode of existence—the female psyche could also make distinctive contributions to historical science. The critical theory of knowledge has demonstrated the shallowness and falsity of the form of realism for which historical knowledge is a maximally faithful and maximally photographic reproduction of the event "as it actually happened," a process whereby immediate reality is poured into the scientific consciousness. We now know that the "event"—which as such is not a possible object of knowledge, but only a possible object of experience—becomes "history" only by means of the action of functions that are defined by the structure and the intentions of the cognitive spirit. The distinctiveness of this definition is responsible for the distinctiveness of the resulting configuration, namely history. This does not mean that there is any sense in which history becomes a "subjective" entity to which the difference between truth and error does not apply. It only means that truth does not rest on the reflective character of the spirit in relation to events. Instead it rests on a certain functional relationship to events, and on the position that ideas, which follow their own laws, at the same time fulfill a demand of the things themselves. Regardless of what this demand might otherwise be, it does not insist that things be photographed by ideas.

At this point, I shall consider only one of the problems stemming from this inevitable dependence of the historical image on the distinctive spiritual structure of the historian. Suppose that historical knowledge were limited to what is ascertained and "experienced" in the strict sense. In that case, the result would be a collection of incoherent fragments. The integral sequences of "history" are possible only on the basis of a continual process of interpolation, a supplementation by means of analogies, and a structuring by reference to developmental concepts. As everyone knows, not even the description of a street fight by eyewitnesses is possible in any other fashion. However, beneath this stratum, in which even the sequences of immediate facts become coherent and meaningful only by virtue of spiritual spontaneity, there is another stratum, which constitutes history and is completely formed by this spontaneity. Suppose that an exhaustive knowledge of all the perceptually ascertainable events in the human world were possible. Even so, all these visible, tangible, and audible phenomena would remain just as indifferent and meaningless as the passing of clouds or the rustling of branches unless we could interpret them psychologically—in other words, locate behind all these external events, thoughts, feelings, and intentions that can never be directly ascertained but can only be conjectured on the basis of the intuitive imagination.

We are not inclined to give any thought to this structure of all history, based as it is on an active and inner recreation of something that always remains beyond experience—for every external phenomenon has historical significance only as the expression of a psyche, only as an effect or a cause of psychic processes. This is because everyday life itself transpires on the basis of the constant use of hypotheses concerning the psychic value of human expressions, and in the domain of everyday life, we generally interpret these expressions with a considerable and self-evident confidence.

This form of psychological interpretation, which is performed exclusively by the cognitive subject of history, rests on a distinctive relationship of identity and difference between this subject and its objects. A certain fundamental identity must obtain. Perhaps an inhabitant of the earth would simply not "understand" an inhabitant of another planet, even if all of the latter's observable behavior were known to him. In general, we understand our own countrymen better than other peoples, members of our family better than strangers, and persons who share our temperament better than those of a contrary disposition. Insofar as comprehension is an inner re-creation of a psychic process that cannot be grasped immediately, we comprehend a spirit to the extent that we resemble it. But this does not amount to a mechanically produced parallelism. One does not need to be a Caesar in order to understand Caesar, nor does one need to be an Augustine in order to understand Augustine. Indeed, a certain differential quality often creates a detachment more favorable for the psychological knowledge of another person than a bias in favor of exactly the same mental constellation.

It is clear that psychological—and thus also historical—understanding is defined by reference to a relationship between its subject and its object that is quite variable and still completely unanalyzed. This relationship certainly cannot be adequately conceived by means of the abstract expression of a purely quantitative mix of identity and difference. On the basis of the foregoing remarks, however, it seems that one point is established: Indisputable facts of observation are consistent with a number of different psychological infrastructures that are in principle unlimited. Within limits—which are, of course, bounded by imaginary and inherently fragmentary constructions—the same external image can produce different inner images in different minds; in other words, images which interpret that external image from the perspective of the mental. In addition, all these inner images can be equally justified. There is no sense in which this is merely a matter of different hypotheses concerning one and the same matter of fact, of which only one can be correct (although naturally this is often enough the case as well). On the contrary, they are related in somewhat the same way as portraits of the same model by different but equally qualified painters. None of them can be said to be "the true" portrait. Rather, each is a complete totality, intrinsically justified, and justified by virtue of its distinctive relationship to the object. Each says something that has no place at all in what the others express, even though it does not contradict them.[1]

Thus the psychological interpretation of men by women may be fundamentally different in many respects from the manner in which women psychologically interpret one another—and the converse is also the case. Goethe once made the apparently paradoxical remark that his idea of women was obviously innate to him and that, *for this reason*, his female characters are all better than those we encounter in reality. For we cannot really presuppose (and Goethe would be the last person to make this assumption) that innate ideas are deceptive. In fact, however, this is more probably a paradoxical expression of the feeling that comprehension of the profound mental nature of another person depends upon the nature of the comprehending subject.

And yet there is also a more general and impersonal experience of persons. There is no sense in which this must always agree with that other experience which is created just as profoundly from our own depths as it penetrates the other person. To the extent that history is applied psychology, it seems to me that the relationships indicated here show that the female nature could be the basis for quite original achievements in history.

Women as such not only have a different mix of identity with and difference from historical objects than men do, and thus the possibility of seeing things men do not see; by virtue of their distinctive psychic structure, they also have the possibility of seeing in a different way. Women interpret existence in general from the standpoint of the a priori of their nature—therefore differently from men, even though these two interpretations are not subject to the simple alternative: true or false. In the same way, through the medium of their psychological interpretation, the historical world could also exhibit another aspect of the relationship between parts and whole. These possibilities may seem problematic and, at this point, important only

1. Concerning all these apriorities of history, see my *The Problems of the Philosophy of History*, chapter 1.

as regards fundamentals. Nevertheless, I think there could be distinctively female functions in historical science, achievements that proceed from the special observational, empathetic, and constructive faculties of the female psyche, whether these are applied to the problem of understanding vague popular movements and undisclosed motivations in personalities or to that of deciphering inscriptions.

The objectivation of the female nature in the artifacts of culture seems most plausible in the domain of art, where certain rudiments of it already exist. In literature, in any case, there is already a group of women who do not have the servile ambition of writing "like a man"; nor do they suggest, by the use of male pseudonyms, that they do not have the faintest notion of the genuinely original and distinctively significant achievement they could make as woman. Of course the eliciting of the female nuance is also quite difficult in literary culture. This is because the general forms of literature are male artifacts (at this point, specifically female *forms* of literature, although perhaps possible, belong in the domain of a utopia). For this reason, there is probably a subtle inner inconsistency between the forms of literature and the specifically female content with which they are filled. Even in lyric poetry written by women, and especially in the instances that are quite successful, I often feel a certain ambivalence between the personal import and the aesthetic form, as if the creative mind and its expression did not have quite the same style. On the one hand, the inner life that attempts to achieve objectivation in an aesthetic form does not quite attain the given limits of this form. And since the requirements of the form must still be fulfilled, this is possible only by means of a certain banality and conventionality. On the other hand, from the perspective of the interiority of life, a residue of emotion and vitality remains unshaped and unreleased. Perhaps this shows that "poetry itself is already a betrayal." For it seems that the two human needs—to disclose oneself and conceal oneself—would be combined in the female psyche in a quite different way than in the male.

Consider the traditional inner forms of lyric poetry: its vocabulary, the domain of expression to which it restricts itself, and the relationship between experience and the expressive symbol. Regardless of the free play that may obtain in individual cases, this is all based on a certain general standard of what it means to reveal one's psychic life: namely, the male standard. Suppose that the female psyche, which in this respect is quite differently tempered, undertakes to express itself in the same forms. On the one hand, a certain insipid quality can easily arise (of course this is also characteristic of much male lyric poetry, even though a connection of the same *generality* does not seem to be responsible for it). On the other hand, the result may be an offensive shamelessness. For some modern female lyric poets, there is a sense in which this is an immanent consequence of the discrepancy between their nature and the traditional style of lyric expression. For others, it is intended to document their freedom from the inner form of femininity.

In some of the published work of the last few years, in any case, I seem to see at least the indistinct beginnings of the formation of a lyric style as the documentation of a distinctive female nature. It is also interesting that on the level of the popular song, there are many peoples in which women are original in the same sense as men, and in this sense at least as productive. This implies that in cultures that are still undeveloped and in cases in which the spirit is not yet objectified, the discrepancy at stake here is not possible. Insofar as cultural forms are still not distinctively and determinately defined, they cannot be definitively male either. As long as these forms remain in an undifferentiated state (corresponding to the greater equality of the male and female among primitive peoples, as established by anthropology), female energies are not under constraint to express themselves in a mode that is not appropriate to them. On the contrary, they are freely formed, and they follow their own norms— which are not yet differentiated from masculine norms, as is now the case.

Here, as in many other developments, the most advanced level reproduces the form of the least advanced. It is probably mathematics, the most sublimated artifact of spiritual culture, that transcends the distinction between male and female more than any other product of the spirit. Its objects provide absolutely no occasion for differential reactions on the part of the intellect. This is the explanation of the fact that women have made a profound impact and significant contributions in mathematics, more so than in all the other sciences. There is a sense in which the abstractness of mathematics *follows* the psychological differentiation of the sexes, in quite the same way that the stage of the production of popular songs *precedes* it.

It seems that the novel poses less serious difficulties for female creativity than the other forms of literature. This is because, as regards both its problem and its aesthetic structure, it has the least rigorous and determinate form. Its boundaries are not strictly limited. Not all the threads the novel spins can be rewoven into its unity. On the contrary, there is a sense in which many strands extend beyond its limits into an indeterminate space. Its unavoidable realism does not permit the novel to liberate itself from the chaos of actuality with the same inflexible rhythm and the same concrete laws of structure that hold for poetry and drama. A male a priori is implicit in the strict forms of poetry and drama from which the informality and the more liberal construction of the novel are free. From the beginning, therefore, the instinct of literary women has attracted them to the novel as their authentic domain. Its form— precisely because it does not qualify as a "form" in a very rigorous sense—is flexible enough to permit some modern novels to become distinctively female creations.

Perhaps the explicit stamp of the female being in characteristically feminine works is in principle most clear in the plastic arts, where an adherence to established traditional standards is superfluous. There is no longer any doubt that all the plastic arts depend upon psychophysical relationships, the manner in which the dynamics of the psyche are transposed into movements of the body, feelings of innervation, and the rhythm of the glance and the touch. Consider the manner—in part immediate, in part reserved—in which the inner life of women becomes visible, their special anatomically and physiologically conditioned way of moving, and their relationship to space, which must follow from the characteristic tempo, scope, and formation of their gestures. In view of all these considerations, we should expect from women a special interpretation and mode of forming phenomena in the plastic arts.

If it holds true for theoretical knowledge that space lies in the psyche, then gestures show that the psyche lies in space. Demeanor is not merely the movement of the body as such but rather movement which is seen as the expression of a psychic process. This is why gesture is one of the most essential bridges and presuppositions of art, the nature of which is that the perceptual is the bearer and manifestation of something that is psychic and spiritual, even if this does not always hold true in the psychological sense. By means of gestures, there is a sense in which a person takes spiritual possession of the part of space that they designate. If we did not move in space, our understanding of space would be very different, or perhaps nonexistent. The manner in which these movements take place is the basis of this understanding.

Naturally, the artist does not mechanically translate his gestures into his work. However, the manner in which he deports himself in space defines—on the basis of many different sorts of transpositions and mediations—his perceptual interpretation of spatial phenomena. Perhaps this becomes clearest in the calligraphic character that was distinctive of East Asian painting. Here the stroke of the brush directly represents the physiological movement of the hand. Its charm lies in the ease, rhythm, and naturalness of the motion of the hand as perceived by the eye.

The distinctive gestures of women exhibit the distinctiveness of their psychic nature most directly in a determinate external expression. Thus it is especially the art of the dance in which woman's innate sense of rhythm has been objectified. In the dance, the schematic character of traditional forms leaves an incomparable scope to the free play of individual impulse, grace, and mode of gesture. I am convinced that if the movements of the real prima ballerinas of the dance were fixed as ornamental lines, we would find that a man could never produce them by any sort of innervation (except by conscious imitation). Until psychophysics and aesthetics advance much further, we can make only the tentative and undemonstrable suggestion that woman's relationship to space is probably different from man's.

This may be just as much a consequence of her transhistorical psychophysical character as of the historical limitation of her sphere of activity to the home. A person's gestures depend upon the spaces in which he or she customarily moves. If we compare the gestures depicted in German paintings of the fifteenth century with those in Italian paintings of the same period, we see the houses of Nuremberg patricians alongside Italian palaces. All of the somewhat restrained, stiff, and ironed-out quality of their gestures—the clothing in which they are garbed looks as if it had lain folded in the bureau too long—suggests the character of persons who are accustomed to movement in confined spaces. However, it seems to me that there is no sense in which the consequences of the circumscription of female movements to the "four walls" are related merely to their constricted space. On the contrary, they are more closely linked with the constant sameness and the habitual character of this milieu.

Because he is occupied "on the outside," in changing spaces that cannot be surveyed and that are less accessible to his own control, the man frequently lacks the wholeness, the unabrasive ease, and the quiet equipoise which constitute that grace which is distinctively feminine. On the other hand, these qualities may develop as a result of continual movement within spaces in which there is nothing left to conquer, spaces which have become nothing more than a corporeal extension of the personality. That is why this is not a matter of purely aesthetic significance. On the contrary, it is probably a special way of sensing space, a special relationship between the nonspatial interior and the spatial perceptuality of motion. As noted above, even though no proof of this is possible now, it seems plausible that in the arts for which the shaping of space is essential, the distinctive relationship to space suggested in the gestures of women would have to be objectified in distinctively female works of art—in quite the same way that the special modes in which the East Asian, the Greek, and the Renaissance man experienced space are precipitated in their artistic styles.

However, the distinctiveness of the female achievement is exhibited quite unambiguously in the art of acting. There is no sense in which this is simply because the role already has a female content. On the contrary, it is a consequence of the deeper nature of the art of acting itself. There is no art in which performance and the totality of the personality are more intimately united. Painting, poetry, and music, of course, have their basis in the total spiritual-corporeal person. However, they conduct the energies of this person into channels that flow in only one direction. At the end, only the performance appears, and much that lies within those energies remains invisible. This holds true even for the art of dance, which suppresses speech, and for the performance of music, in which concrete per-

ceptuality is irrelevant. In these arts, the separation of the actual
creative moment from the artifact that exists independent of this
moment constitutes the temporal expression of this phenomenon.

Acting, on the other hand, can admit no possible interval between
the process and the product of the performance. In this case, both its
subjective and its objective aspects coincide absolutely in a single
existential moment. As a result, they provide the correlate or the
protoform for that unconditional entry of the total personality into
the aesthetic phenomenon. If there is anything that qualifies as a
definition of the female nature, it corresponds to this aspect of the
nature of acting. This is because—and here I must reiterate a point
made above—the innumerable observations concerning the distinctive character of the female psyche may be summarized as follows:
For the woman, the ego and its activity, and the center of the
personality and its periphery, are much more closely fused than for
the man. The woman translates the inner process—insofar as its
concealment is not required by morality or self-interest—more immediately into its expression. This results in the characteristic coherence which is responsible for the fact that psychic changes in women
become physical changes much more easily than is the case for men.

This is the most profound reason—and we shall be concerned with
it later—why women generally fail in the creation of objective
culture: They do not translate their activity into an objective entity
that continues to exist independent of that activity. The estuary of
the current that forms their inner vitality springs directly from its
source. This quite often is interpreted as a deficiency. However,
since it constitutes a positive and autonomous mode of being antithetical to the male's, that is an error. In the art of acting, it is the
innermost structure of the performance. The performance only has
access to a single moment in which interior and exterior, the sudden
occurrence of the central impulse and the phenomenon that it presents, cannot be severed, and the result of the activity cannot be
objectified independent of the activity itself.

The intimate relationship between all the aspects of her nature
does not, as we are so often told, constitute the woman as a subjective being, but rather as a being for whom the distinction between
the subjective and the objective really does not exist. There is a sense
in which this intimate relationship also defines the aesthetic and

thoroughly trans-subjective "idea" of the art of acting, in which—separated by no temporal, spatial, or substantive hiatus—the inner life is responsible for its own visible and audible expression. Thus it is no accident that the Latin peoples, to whom an instinct—obviously quite difficult to substantiate—has always ascribed a character that is in some sense female, are the truly theatrical peoples.

The art of acting comprises an interweaving of ultimate components that also places it in a different and quite fundamental relationship to the female nature. The dramatic poem represents the continuous movement of a destiny inexorably determined by its own inner logic. When the actor embodies this destiny, his rendition is not a mere transposition of the poet's language into a tangible medium that is complete and natural. On the contrary, the rendition itself is a work of art governed by its own norms of value. In this work of art, what might be called the uninterrupted flow of the inner event of the drama is decomposed into a sequence of perceptual images of more or less considerable duration and subject to an aesthetic law. In this manner, the categories of being and becoming are brought into harmony in a distinctive fashion. The eternal turmoil of fate is grasped in the timeless silence of art, in the dramatic scene as a whole as well as in the phenomenon of the individual actor.

This harmony can be modulated in different ways. The emphasis can lie more on the process of becoming—in other words, on fate and activity. Or it may lie more on being, on what might be called the concrete perceptual cross-section drawn through the fate that always comes to pass. If the stress lies more on the latter aspect, the performance will correspond more closely to the female nature. In that case, the claim that objective culture makes upon the woman—the demand that she accomplish what the man cannot—will be more adequately fulfilled. This is why one of our most knowledgeable theoreticians of the drama has emphasized the point that when women play active dramatic roles that set the process of fate in motion, they are always endowed with male qualities.

At this point, a discussion of the question of "beauty" is called for. This seems to be a departure from our subject matter, but in fact it is intimately related to the most profound cultural significance of the woman. In spite of the offensive banality that designates women as "the fair sex," it still contains a significant point. Suppose that there is a polarity of constitutive values, one representing the power-hungry and form-determining relationship to a real or ideal external entity, the other representing a self-contained existence in which all the existential elements are modulated by reference to its own inner harmony. The first value might be called "significance" and the second "beauty." Significance is, of course, a state of being. But it is a transitive state that breaks through its own boundaries as performance, achievement, knowledege, or efficacy. Regardless of its autonomy in other respects, its standard of value is determined on the basis of this relationship.

Suppose we reduce the countless norms that historically qualify as "male"—in other words, norms that are independent of a general human ethic—to an abstract expression. Then they may be formulated as the requirement that the man should be "significant," where this word must naturally eliminate all the capricious turns of linguistic usage. If, in conformity with this, the historical "female" norm is epitomized in the demand that the woman should be beautiful, then this also holds true in the comprehensive and abstract sense; for example, it naturally rejects any restriction of beauty to a pretty face. The claim that a crippled old woman can be "beautiful" does not violate the concept at all, since in its full sense, this concept signifies the self-contained completeness of the total being. This is responsible for the relationship between the work of art—the most complete of all human productions—and "beauty," a relationship which is, of course, often misconstrued: the unity of the interior and the exterior with the many forms of its symbolism, which are quite intricate; and the capacity—in spite of its dependent existence—always to remain in a state of self-sufficient repose.

The man externalizes himself. His energy is discharged into his performance. Thus he "signifies" something that is in some sense independent of him, either dynamically or ideally, in a creative or a representative fashion. The constitutive idea of the woman, on the other hand, is the unbroken character of her periphery, the organic finality in the harmony of the aspects of her nature, both in their relationship to one another and in the symmetry of their relationship to their center. This is precisely what epitomizes the beautiful. In the symbolism of metaphysical concepts, the woman represents being and man represents becoming. This is why the man must establish his significance in a particular substantive area or in an idea, in a historical or cognitive world. However, the woman should be beautiful in the sense that this represents "bliss in itself."

Of course this relationship between the female principle and the principle of beauty (here it can be said that the latter is not conceived as a value but simply as an existential configuration) is also exhibited in physical appearance for its own sake. The grounds on which Schopenhauer bases his claim that the male body has a higher degree of beauty do not seem adequate to me. Here, too, the male can qualify more as that which *signifies*. The more pronounced definition of the muscles which are good for work, the obvious functional character of the anatomical structure, the expression of force together with what might be called the aggressive angularity of forms—all this is not so much the expression of beauty as of significance: in other words, the possibility of emerging from oneself and making effective contact with an external entity.

The "functional" character of the *female* body is not based on this sort of contact but rather on a more passive function, or a function the exercise of which lies beyond both activity and passivity. The smooth face, the lack of the paltry sexual organs that interrupt the flow of the lines of the body, the symmetrically molded cushions of fat—all this orients the female body much more to the stylistic ideal of "beauty" than to the active ideal of "significance." Rounded forms are more appropriate to the former ideal than angular forms because they make perceptible the relationship to a center that is uniformly coherent throughout, and thereby also to the immanent completeness in which the female nature finds its symbolic expression. Thus the quality of beauty is more closely related to the female phenomenon than to the male, even if only in the sense that the woman possesses a greater natural disposition to beauty. The same sort of point holds for the domain of the psyche. It is certainly not the case that all women are "beautiful souls." However, woman's psychic structure is grounded in the intention of this harmonious form of existence: The contradictions of the male life are resolved into their unity, as if automatically; and the idea of this form of existence is translated into the reality of her life. As a result, it is almost always only in women that this idea is empirically realized.

In the same way, the work of art possesses the magic power of binding together value sequences which in empirical reality are independent and unrelated into a self-evident unity. Perhaps its most profound nature lies in this capacity. Thus the actor ties together the dramatic event and concrete perceptual beauty—two sequences that intrinsically have absolutely nothing to do with one another—into a single aesthetic unity. With the exception of the dance, which is related to acting in this respect, there is no art in which beauty is so immediately required from the actual personal performance, and not from its result—regardless of whether the statics of the instant or the smoothness of gestures are at stake. Insofar as the tranquillity of pictoral beauty embraces the impetuosity of action and the event, the distinctive phenomenon of "grace" arises. The male actor transposes this demand more into the value domain of significance. However, by virtue of the law of her nature, the actress (regardless of the extent to which this demand applies to her) is already disposed to realize the theatrical synthesis by incorporating the dramatic contents into this law.

Within the general areas of culture, I shall not pursue any further the question of the possible provinces in which women demonstrate a creativity that men lack, an inquiry the defines the sense in which women contribute to the advance of objective culture. On the contrary, I shall now take up the two areas of female achievement in which women exercise—or allegedly exercise—a creative cultural impact on a grand scale: the home and the influence of women upon men.

As regards the "home," even when the highest values are ascribed to it, actually they are always linked to the specific achievements of the home, but not to the general category of life it represents. A series of the most important of all cultural entities exhibits the following distinctive pattern. On the one hand, such an entity is one part of the totality of life and is coordinated with other domains of life that are defined by their own essential form. Both in combination with these other domains and in reciprocal interaction with them, it determines the totality of our individual, societal, and spiritual existence. On the other hand, each such entity constitutes a *total* world: in other words, a form in which the contents of life as such are comprehended and in which they are structured, treated, and experienced according to a special law. From the first standpoint, the structure of our existence appears as a sum of interwoven and formed contents. From the second, there is a sense in which it appears as a sum of worlds, each of which comprehends the same existential content in a distinctive form or a form that represents a totality.

This holds true for religion, art, the practical affairs of everyday life, and knowledge. Each is an aspect of life. In varying combinations as principal and subsidiary factors, they form the unity of a total individual as well as that of public existence. However, each of them is also a *total* world. In other words, all of the contents of life can be experienced under the aspect of their religious significance; the totality of things is in principle subject to the formative possibilities of art; everything the world presents to us can become an object of the practical-ethical attitude; and the domain of the given as such constitutes both the fulfillment and the task of knowledge.

The empirical realization of worlds formed in this way on the basis of an a priori formal law is obviously quite fragmentary. The domain of the force of such a formal law is always limited by the given historical situation, and the comprehension of contents is restricted by the finite powers and lifespan of individuals. In principle, however, there are as many total worlds as there are forms of this sort. In order to be experienced, every content must fall under one or another of these forms. Independent of them, such a content can be expressed only as an abstract idea.

With certain limitations, there are also more concrete entities that function in the same way as these forms. Consider, for example, the state. Within the totality of a single life, even one maximally committed to the state, it is never more than one element among others that belong to other formative spheres of our existence. On the other hand, the state can qualify as a universally comprehensive form. Its organization and sphere of influence can somehow embrace all the possible contents of life, regardless of the varying degrees in which historical states realize this logical possibility.

Finally, the "home" functions in this double category as well. It is also one existential factor in the life of its inhabitants. They also have personal and religious, social and intellectual interests. Regardless of how important or minimal these interests may be, they still extend beyond the "home." On the basis of the "home" and these other interests, its inhabitants build their lives together. But the home is also a distinctive mode in which the *total* contents of life are formed. At least within the more advanced culture of Europe, there is no interest, no gain or loss of either an internal or an external sort, and no domain somehow affected by individuals that does not, together with all the other interests, merge into the unique synthesis of the home, none that would not somehow be deposited here. The home is an aspect of life and at the same time a special way of forming, reflecting, and interrelating the totality of life.

To have accomplished this is the immense cultural achievement of woman. The home is an objective entity whose distinctiveness can be compared with no other. It has been stamped by the special abilities and interests, and emotionality and intellectuality, of the woman, by the total rhythm of her being. Of course each of the two meanings of the home—as a part and as a whole—holds true for both sexes. However, their dimensions are distributed in such a way that, for the man, the home signifies more a part of life as such; for the woman, it signifies more the distinctively constituted totality of life. For this reason, the meaning of the home is not exhausted—either objectively or for the woman—by any one of its single functions, including its function with respect to children. On the contrary, it is an autonomous value and purpose, analogous to the work of art in the following respect: Although it is true that the entire subjective cultural significance of the work of art depends upon what it produces for consumers, nevertheless it also has an independent meaning, which is objective with reference to its own perfection and its own laws alone.

The fact that the cultural formation of the home as described here often remains unclear is a consequence of the fluid and variable particulars of the phenomenon, which are there to serve the interests of persons and everyday matters. As a result, the objective cultural significance of the *form* in which the home consummates the synthesis of these fluid and fleeting performances is overlooked. In any case, consider what the home possesses beyond the sum of its ephemeral achievements and as their real configuration of stable values, composed of influences, memories, and the organization of life. All this is linked with the variable and personal life of the hour and the year in a more radical fashion than holds true for the objective cultural achievements of a male provenance.

At this point—and naturally with a further degree of abstraction—one might draw attention to a general human correlation. The dualistic, restless nature of the male, subject to the uncertainty of becoming (for the male nature, beyond the domain of its individual variations, can be described in this way in contrast to the female nature), demands release in objectified activity. Consider all the fluctuating and differentiated features of the process of culture with which the man has developed himself from the ground up, out of natural existence. There is a sense in which these features produce their counterweight in the abiding, objective, trans-individual artifacts to which the cultural work of the male as such, whether he be a king or a wagon driver, tends. One might conclude that the human being in general needs a certain combination or proportion of these two fundamental tendencies: becoming and being, differentiation and coherence, surrender to the temporal process of things and release from this process into an ideal or substantial realm. Even with abstractions of this sort, these oppositions are not expressed with complete clarity. They are the formal elements of the nature of the human, and they can be grasped by consciousness only within some particular material in which they function.

The way they are combined in the female type is the exact antithesis of their combination in the male type just described. We experience the woman not so much in terms of the idea of becoming as in terms of being, regardless of how imprecise and vague this concept may be. The integral, natural, and self-contained quality which distinguishes the female nature from the male probably finds its most abstract category here. On the other hand, it finds its "counter-model"—and thereby that equilibrium of the general human existence—in the contents of female activity. They are fleeting and committed to individual contingencies; they come and go with the demands of the moment; they do not represent the construction of a cultural world that is in any sense permanent and impersonal. On the contrary, they stand in the service of the lives and the persons that can develop from this structure.

The same correlation, but somewhat more specific, lies in the fact that the woman in comparison with the man—who is, so to say, the born transgressor of limits—appears as the self-contained being, circumscribed within rigid limits. However, her aesthetic achievements fail precisely where the strict definition of form prevails: in drama, musical composition, and architecture. With the reservation that these conceptual symmetries do not qualify as static constructs but as a mere nucleus, implicated in the interplay of thousands of changes, it seems that the nature of the sexes and the process of their authentication have exchanged roles. The deepest nature of one sex lies in an unceasing process of becoming and expansive activity. It is inextricably implicated in the temporal interplay of a most profound dualism. Its authentication, however, takes place in the domain of the objective, the continuous, the substantial. The other sex is concentric with itself. It reposes within its own meaning. As regards its authentication, however, it is devoted to the fleeting experience. It is not oriented to any result that could not be re-incorporated into this flux of actual interests and claims.

The home possesses the following distinctive structure: In its state of serene, self-contained completeness (at least this is what its idea implies), all the lines of the cosmos of culture transpire in an inner unity that is concrete and continuous. In this way, it assumes that real and symbolic relationship to the nature of the woman by means of which it could become her great cultural achievement.

The other cultural significance which has been ascribed to the woman is structured on the basis of a quite different principle. The original and objective cultural accomplishment of women allegedly lies in the fact that, for the most part, they have formed the male psyche. Consider, for example, the extent to which the fact of pedagogy, the legal influence that persons have on one another, or the crafting of his material by an artist all belong to objective culture. To that same extent they are due to the influences and the formative and transformative activities of women, thanks to whom the male psyche is what it is. In the formation of this psyche, women allegedly express themselves. They create an objective entity that is possible only by means of their agency—in the sense that it is possible to speak of human creativity at all, which invariably designates nothing more than a resultant of the creative force and the distinctive powers and determinants of its object. The work of the woman, so it might be claimed in this connection, is the man; for in fact men would be different than they are were it not for the influence of women upon them. This line of reasoning argues, further, that the conduct and the activity of men—in short, the whole of male culture—is in part based on the influence, or, as this is expressed, on the "stimulus" provided by women.

However, there is a lack of clarity here. Regardless of how powerful this "influence" may be, it becomes significant for objective
culture only insofar as, in men, it is transposed into those results that
correspond to the *male* mode of being and that can be produced
only in this mode of being. This is radically different from every
mode of cultural production whose contents are transposed into
other contents in such a way that the former may provoke diverse
effects only in the latter. Our culture is male not only with respect to
its contingent contents but also with respect to its form as objective
culture. Suppose that the active bearers of this culture experience
influences, no matter how profound, from women. There is no sense
in which this makes the culture as such "female," no more than a
culture of the southern latitudes, where the warm climate decisively
influences the activities, tendencies, and contents of the lives of its
bearers, thereby qualifies as a "warm culture."

This doctrine of the "indirect" cultural significance of the woman
commits a profound categorial error: that of confusing the transmission of a substantive and spiritual content (which may then have a
further impact on the life-process of the recipient) with a direct
influence on this life itself, which is not mediated by a content that is
in some sense timeless and ideally separable from its bearer. In all
human relations, from the most fleeting to the historically most
important, this difference—obviously with all of its innumerable
practical compounds—obtains: whether one subject acts upon
another as the sunshine makes a plant grow or as a storm tears out its
roots—that is, by producing a result that is not in any respect pre-
figured in the object acted upon, cause and effect being linked by no
sort of *substantive equivalence*; or whether this sort of equivalence
does obtain between them, an artifact retaining its identity like a gift,
but also like a spiritual entity, not ceasing to belong to one person
because it comes into the possession of another. In the former case,
an effect of life is transmitted, in the latter case a content of life. The
former may often be the more profound, carrying the mysteries of
the ultimately moving experiences and transformations of life from
one person to another. But the latter is the genuine cultural phenomenon. It constitutes man as a historical being and the heir of the
creations of his race. It exhibits the fact that the human being is the
objective being. In this case alone, the person receives something
that the other possessed or possesses. In the former case, however, he

receives something that the giver himself does not possess, something that becomes a new entity solely as a consequence of the nature
and energies of the recipient. The action of one person on another is
exempt from simple causality—where there is a sense in which the
effect is morphologically indifferent to the cause—under the following condition alone: In the spirit, the process of life is distinguished
from its content. This is the basis of the first and last possibility of
culture. As a result, it is possible for the recipient to possess what the
giver offers, not merely its effects.

These two senses of "effect" are conflated by the theory that
identifies the cultural achievement of women with their effect upon
men. This theory cannot really mean that a content which women
have created is transmitted to men. Even the "moderation of customs," which might be mentioned here, is much less a consequence
of the influence of women than an effect of the banal fact of
tradition. Neither the abolition of slavery at the beginning of the
Middle Ages nor the later abolition of serfdom, neither the humani-
zation of the practices of war and the treatment of the defeated nor
the elimination of torture, neither the introduction of poverty wel-
fare on a grand and effective scale nor the elimination of the right of
self-defense can be traced, as far as we know, to female influences.
On the contrary, the elimination of meaningless cruelties is directly
due to an objectivation of life, an objectification that frees what is
instrumentally purposive from all the impulsiveness, excesses, and
myopia of the subject.

It is true that pure objectivity (in the money economy, for example) brings with it a certain severity and ruthlessness that may not
appear in affairs that are more personal and thus more emotionally
determined. However, the "moderation of customs" is not a consequence of this factor but rather of purely objective developments of
the spirit, which represent the distinctively male character of culture.
The type of activity in which one person gives another what he
himself does not have is realized most forcefully in the relationship
of women to men. The life, even the spirituality, of countless men
would be different and more impoverished if they did not receive
something from women. But what they receive is not a content that
already existed in this way in women. On the other hand, what men

give to the spiritual life of women tends to correspond to this sort of case. Paradoxically expressed, what women give is something that cannot be communicated, a way of existing that remains within them. When it impinges upon the man, it releases something in him that phenomenologically bears no resemblance at all to this way of existing itself. It becomes "culture" only in the man. Only with this reservation can it be claimed that women "stimulate" male cultural achievements. In a more direct sense, however, which includes the content of culture itself, this is not the case. One cannot possibly call Rachel the "stimulator" of Jacob's work, any more than one can claim that in this sense Dulcinea of Toboso "stimulated" the deeds of Don Quixote or Ulrike von Levetzow the *Marienbad Elegy*.

On the whole, therefore, the home remains the supreme cultural achievement of women. This is because, as discussed above, the unique structure of the home as a category of life makes it possible for beings who are in general quite remote from the objectivation of their life to consummate this process to the greatest extent possible, precisely in the home. To a preeminent degree, household management falls under the cultural category of "secondary originality" that was stressed at the beginning of this essay. Typical purposes and general forms of realization are delineated in the home. In every case, however, both are dependent on individual variability, spontaneous decisions, and a responsibility that applies only to unrepeatable situations. Thus the occupation of the housewife—in all its diverse qualities, it is still governed by a thoroughly unified meaning—is an intermediate entity, lying between production out of the supremely creative self and the mere repetition of prescribed forms of activity. This determines its position in the social scale of values.

There is a series of male occupations which, although they require no specific talents, are still not inferior. They are not necessarily creative and individual, yet they do not exclude the individual from any social status. This holds true for law, for example, and for many commercial occupations. The occupation of housewife is also a case of this sort of social formation. It can be filled by anyone of merely average abilities, yet it is not subaltern, or at least it does not have to be. An observation, long since trivial, must be repeated here. Consider the modern development, which rules out the occupation of

housewife for an increasing number of women and renders it intrinsically empty for others. Consider the aversion to marriage on the
part of men, the difficulties for marriage produced by the individualization of both partners, the limitation of the number of children,
and the expatriation of countless productive activities out of the
home. As a result of these factors, the activity stratum of secondary
originality becomes increasingly closed to women, with the result
that they are forced into the alternative between the very high and
the very demeaning occupations: the most advanced and spiritually
productive professions, which require talents that are always quite
exceptional, and the inferior occupations, which remain beneath
their social and personal aspirations. With very few exceptions, only
the occupation of housewife is open to them as a pendant to the legal
career, which is unspecific without being subaltern. The supposition
that the occupation of schoolteacher qualifies as such a case is a
serious misunderstanding, which can be explained only as a consequence of the pressing need for such an intermediate occupation. In
reality, teaching requires distinctive talents in quite the same way as
any scientific or artistic activity does.

If this is the situation from the perspective of the actual historical
facts, then it is obviously much more difficult to assess the future
prospects of a culture that is objectively female: the production of
those contents that men are, in principle, incapable of producing.
Suppose that the new freedom of mobility to which the woman
aspires leads to an *objectivation of the female nature* in the same way
that, thus far, culture has constituted an objectivation of the male
nature. Suppose that it does not result in substantively equivalent
reproductions of male culture by women (the value of this process is
not my problem here). In that case, of course, a new continent of
culture would be discovered. The ideal of the women's movement
cannot be an "independent humanity"—as it has been characterized
from another standpoint—but rather an "independent femininity."
This is because, as a result of the historical identification of the male
and the human, that humanity, regarded from the standpoint of its
content, would appear as masculinity. All aspirations of this sort
ultimately proceed from the idea that women want to become and
to possess what men are and possess. Here I shall not disparage the

value of this aspiration. From the standpoint of objective culture, however, we should not examine this value but rather an autonomous *femininity*: in other words, the differentiation of the distinctively female from the immediacy of the transitory process of life in its autonomy as a real and ideal entity.

As regards this ideal, we could, of course, go so far as to suppose that its polar antithesis is the *most immediate* condition for its realization: the mechanical leveling of education, rights, occupations, and conduct. Consider the fact that the achievement and the position of women vis-à-vis men have remained in a relationship of gross inequality for so long, with the result that the development of a distinctively female objectivity has been obstructed. In view of this consideration, we might suppose that it is first necessary to pass through the opposite extreme of extravagant equality before the new synthesis—an objective culture enriched with the nuance of the female—could develop beyond this state. In the same way, there are extreme individualists today who advocate socialism because they think that a truly natural ranking and a new aristocracy that would really qualify as the rule of the *best* is to be expected only as a result of the transition through a leveling process produced by socialism.

At this point, I shall discuss neither the paths to an objective female culture nor the quantum of their contents that might have a chance of realization. However, a formal problem that cannot be overlooked remains in the stratum of principles. It is a problem to which all aspects of the foregoing discussions have been driven, as if to the most profound and ultimately decisive issue: the question of whether the objectivation of its contents does not contradict the innermost essence of the distinctively female existence. It is the question of whether the same fallacy that has been criticized so often here has perhaps already been committed by posing this question and imposing this demand: the fallacy of imposing on the female nature a criterion of performance that is grounded in the distinctively different masculine nature. The concept of objective culture seemed to be so abstract that, even if historically it had been realized only by male contents, the idea of a future female realization of its contents could still be possible. But perhaps objective culture—not only as regards its heretofore existing content but purely as a form of

authentication simpliciter—is so heterogeneous vis-à-vis the female
nature that the idea of an objective female culture is a contradiction
in terms.

No one will deny that individual women do or can succeed in
creating artifacts of objective culture. But this still does not decide
the issue of whether the feminine as such—that which does not lie
within the capacity of any man—is objectified in such artifacts. The
claim that we can recognize the person in his works holds true only
with very powerful reservations. Sometimes we are more than our
work. Sometimes—paradoxical as this sounds—our work is more
than we are. Sometimes one is remote from the other, or they
coincide only in fortuitous respects. The question of whether the
integral nature of the woman has really achieved the status of "objective spirit" in any cultural configuration—with the exception of the
home and its unique structure—cannot be answered with complete
certainty. In light of this consideration, it is, of course, all the more
probable that the distinctively female culture has been blocked not
by the contingencies of individual cultural contents and their historical development but rather by a fundamental discrepancy between
the form of the female nature and the form of objective culture as
such.

The more radically the male and female natures diverge from one
another in this way, the less the denigration of women, which is
usually inferred from this split, follows from it. Moreover, the female
world emerges all the more autonomously on the basis of a completely distinctive foundation that is neither shared with the male
world nor derived from it. Obviously, numerous commonalities can
arise on this basis, for there is no sense in which everything a person
does and experiences develops from the ultimate ground of masculinity or femininity.

From the standpoint of cultural history, consider the extreme
point that the ideal of the independence and equality of women
seems to be capable of reaching: an objective female culture parallel
to the male and thereby annulling its brutal historical idealization.
Here this point is superceded as well, and in the same direction.
Under these circumstances, the male monopolization of objective
culture would persist, but with justification. This is because objective culture as a formal principle would qualify as a one-sided male

principle. Juxtaposed to it, the female form of existence would present itself as a different form, autonomous on the basis of its ultimate essence, incommensurable on the basis of the standard of the male principle, and with contents that are not formed in the same way. Thus its meaning would no longer turn on an equivalence *within* the general form of objective culture but rather on an equivalence between two modes of existence that have a completely different rhythm. One is dualistic, oriented to becoming, knowledge, and volition. As a result, it objectifies the contents of its life out of the process of life in the form of a cultural world. The other lies beyond this subjectively constituted and objectively developed dichotomy. For this reason, the contents of its life are not experienced in a form that is external to them. On the contrary, it must search out a perfection that is immanent to them.

For this reason, the claim might be rejected that women possess their own *world*, which, from its very fundamentals, is incomparable with the world of the male. Suppose that the female nature is understood in the radical sense that proposes to describe not the individual woman but rather the principle of her nature, the sense that admits the equivalence between the objective and the male in order to repudiate the equivalence between the male and the human all the more fundamentally. In that case, the female consciousness may not constitute a "world" at all, because a "world" is a form of the contents of consciousness, established through the inclusion of these contents in a totality in which every part lies outside every other, and the sum of these parts in some sense lies outside the self. A world, therefore, is the ideal of a self which can never be completely realized and whose transcendental function consists in proceeding beyond and developing outside itself. Thus, as a transcendental category, it would not come into question where the metaphysical nature of the psyche is not oriented in the dualistic-objectivistic direction, but is rather conclusively defined in a consummate state of being and life itself.

THE RELATIVE AND THE ABSOLUTE
IN THE PROBLEM OF THE SEXES

In all the areas of inner existence, as well as in those that arise from the cognitive and practical relationship of the inner self to the world, we invariably grasp the meaning and value of a single element in its relationship—or, rather, *as* its relationship—to another element. Moreover, the nature of this latter element is also determined by reference to the former. The two elements do not remain in this condition of relativity, however; rather, one of them, alternating with the other, develops into an absolute that sustains or governs the relationship. All of the great dichotomies of the spirit—the self and the world, subject and object, the individual and society, stability and motion, material and form, and many others—have experienced this fate: Each aspect develops a comprehensive and profound meaning on the basis of which it encompasses both its own limited significance and its polar antithesis as well.

The fundamental relativity in the life of our species lies in the relationship between masculinity and femininity; this relationship also exhibits the typical process whereby one of a pair of relative elements becomes absolute. We assess the achievements and commitments, the intensity and structural forms of the male and female nature by reference to certain norms. But these norms are not neutral and detached from the opposition between the sexes. On the contrary, they themselves are of a male nature.

At this point I shall not take up the exceptions, reversals, and further developments of this relationship. Consider patriotism and the demands of art, general morality and specific social ideas, the equitability of practical judgment and the objectivity of theoretical knowledge, the power and the profundity of life. As regards their form and their claim, there is a sense in which these categories are generally human. As regards their actual historical formation, however, they are thoroughly male. If we call those ideas which appear as absolute the objective simpliciter, then following equation holds in the historical life of our species: the objective = the male. Consider the general human tendency, probably anchored in profound metaphysical grounds, for one member of a pair of dichotomous concepts, the meaning and value of which are conjointly determined, to acquire preeminence. As a result, this member, which now has an absolute significance, comprehends and dominates the entire interplay of reciprocity or equilibrium. In the fundamental relationship of human sexuality, this tendency has created a historical paradigm for itself.

The male sex is not merely superior in relation to the female but acquires the status of the *generally human*, governing the phenomena of the individual male and the individual female in the same way. In various media, this fact is grounded in the *power position* of men. If we express the historical relationship between the sexes quite grossly as that between master and slave, then it is one of the privileges of the master that he does not always need to think about the fact that he is master. The position of the slave, on the other hand, ensures that he will never forget his status. There is no doubt that the woman loses a conscious sense of her being as a female much more rarely than holds true for the man and his being as a male. There are innumerable occasions on which the man appears to think in a purely objective fashion without his masculinity concurrently occupying any place in his perceptions. On the other hand, it seems as if the woman never loses the feeling—which may be more or less clear or obscure—that she is a woman. This forms the subterranean ground of her life that never entirely disappears. All the contents of her life transpire on its basis.

The differential, male moment in ideational images and normative positions, in works and emotional complexes, disappears much more easily from the consciousness of its bearers than the corresponding female moment does. In the activities of his life, the man as master does not take as vital an interest in his relationship to the female as the woman must take in her relationship to the male. As a result, the expressions of the male nature are easily transposed for us into the sphere of trans-specific, neutral objectivity and validity (to which the specifically male quality, should it be noticed, is subordinated as an individual and contingent matter). This is exhibited in the endlessly repeated phenomenon that certain judgments, institutions, aspirations, and interests which men naively regard as simply objective are perceived by women as thoroughly and characteristically male.

Another tendency that is based on the foundation of male dominance produces the same result. From time immemorial, every domination that rests on a subjective preponderance of force has made it its business to provide itself with an objective justification: in short, to transform might into right. The history of politics, the priesthood, forms of the economy, the law of the family, all these are full of examples of this process. Suppose that the will of the *pater familias* which is imposed upon the home appears as "authority." In that case he is no longer an arbitrary exploiter of power but rather is the embodiment of an objective law that is concerned with the trans-personal and general interests of the family itself. On the basis of this analogy, and often even in this connection, there is a sense in which the psychological superiority that is secured for expressions of the male nature by the relationship of domination between men and women develops into a logical superiority. These expressions of the male nature claim normative significance on the ground that they exhibit the objective truth and rectitude that are equally valid for everyone, male or female.

The fact that the masculine is absolutized in this way as the objective simpliciter and the impartial standard of authority applies not only to the empirically given actuality of the masculine. On the contrary, it also has the result that the ideas and ideal demands that develop both from and for the masculine acquire the status of trans-sexual absolutes. This has fateful consequences for the valuation of women. On the one hand, it is the source of the mystifying overestimation of women. Suppose, however, we come to believe, in spite of everything, that existence is grounded in a completely independent and normative basis. If there is no criterion for this existence, then the possibility is opened for every sort of hyperbole and indefinite limit in the face of the unknown and the misunderstood.

On the other hand, and more obviously, all misunderstandings and underestimations are a consequence of judging a being according to criteria that are created for an antithetical being. On this basis, the autonomy of the female principle *cannot* be acknowledged at all. As long as this issue simply concerns a brutalization of the manifestations of the female nature (as regards both its reality and its value) by the manifestations of the male nature that lie on the same level, there is still hope for an appeal to a spiritual court of justice that lies beyond both male and female. However, if this higher court of appeal itself is masculine, then it is not at all clear how the female nature could ever be judged by reference to norms that apply to it.

Suppose that in this way women—their accomplishments, convictions, and the practical and theoretical contents of their lives—encounter the absolute standard (which is formed by the criteria that are valid for men). At the same time, this absolute standard is juxtaposed or opposed to a relative standard that is no less a consequence of the male prerogative and often imposes demands that are antithetical to it. This is because the man requires from the woman what is pleasing to him in his capacity as a self-interested party and in his polar relationship to her. This is the feminine in the traditional sense. It does not signify a self-sufficient and self-contained character. On the contrary, it is oriented to the man—to what is intended to please, serve, and complement him. Because the male prerogative imposes this duality of standards on women—the masculine as the trans-sexually objective, and the specifically female standard that is directly correlated with and often diametrically opposed to this—there is actually no standpoint from which women can be unconditionally valued. Thus the mockingly critical attitude toward women is so pervasive—and at the same time so cheap and banal—for the following reason: As soon as they are esteemed from the standpoint of one of these critical spheres, the polar antithesis appears, on the basis of which they must actually be denigrated.

And now this duality of mutually exclusive claims—in a sense, retaining their form and altering only their dimensions—is continued within the domain of the inner needs with which the man as an individual resorts to the woman. Suppose that the male is the being that is determined, in both an internal and an external sense, by and for the division of labor. The more profound consequences of this idea will not appear until later. In that case, the individual man who has become one-sided as a result of the division of labor will try to find the completion of his one-sided qualities in the woman. In her, therefore, he will also seek a differentiated being who has to achieve this completion in the most diverse ways imaginable, extending from an approximate equivalence to a radical opposition. The specificity in the content of the individual personality demands from the woman a specificity of content that is correlated with it. At the same time, however, differentiation as a form of life in general also requires its complement and correlation: namely, the homogeneous being, wherever possible accentuated with reference to no particularly stressed content at all, and rooted in the undifferentiated ground of nature. It is the fate of a highly differentiated process of individualization that it makes these two mutually exclusive claims, often with the same force: on the one hand, upon another being that is just as definitively individualized, but with an opposite character and content; on the other hand, upon the annulment, in principle, of such an individualized being.

At any given time, the specific content and the general form of the male life require for their completion, their harmony, and their release two correlates that are diametrically opposed. It is often the problematic—or even the more or less fully developed tragedy—of relationships that the man regards the fulfillment of one of these requirements by the woman as self-evident and allows his consciousness to be completely dominated by the absence of the other, which logically cannot exist at the same time as the former. To act as a thoroughly differentiated, individualized being, and at the same time to act as a unity containing in some deep stratum the forces of all differentiated qualities in a state of complete diffuseness: this ability seems to be given only to those women who are gifted with the genius of femininity. It is comparable to the great work of art whose effect is produced in precisely this duality. Moreover, it is indifferent to the conceptual incompatibility of this duality. In typical cases, however, the woman is the being in relation to whom the man has the right to make demands and to pass judgments from the pinnacle of objective norms.

Nevertheless, the development, both external and in the history of culture, indicated in all these considerations is probably grounded in the trans-historical basis of the sexual difference. The decisive motive of the entire sphere of phenomena is that indicated above. The difference between the sexes appears to be a relationship between two logically equivalent and polar parties. Typically, however, the relationship is more important for the woman than for the man. It is more essential to her that she is a woman than for the man that he is a male. For the man, there is a sense in which sexuality is something he does. For the woman, it is a mode of being. And yet—or, rather, precisely for this reason—the significance of the sexual *difference* is only a secondary fact for the woman. She reposes in her femininity as if in an absolute substantial essence and—somewhat paradoxically expressed—indifferent to whether men exist or not. For the man, this centripetal and autonomous sexuality simply does not exist. His masculinity (in the sexual sense) is much more pervasively bound up with his relationship to the woman than the femininity of the woman is determined by her relationship to the man. The naive presupposition (which is precisely what is at stake here) is an obstacle to the acknowledgment of this consideration, and perhaps even to its comprehension: the assumption that femininity is a phenomenon determined only by its relation to the man, and that if this relation no longer obtained, nothing would remain. In fact, what remains is not a neutral "human being" but a woman. The autonomy of the sexual in the woman is exhibited most extensively in the course of pregnancy, which is independent of any further relationship to the man, and also in the consideration that, in the prehistory of humanity, obviously a very long time passed before there was any recognition of the causation of pregnancy by the sexual act.

The woman lives in the most profound identity of being and being-a-woman, in the absoluteness of *immanently* defined sexuality, the characteristic essence of which does not require the relationship to the other sex. Considered from another angle, this fact of course makes the singular historical phenomenon of precisely this relationship—in a sense the sociological locus of her metaphysical nature—especially important to her. The distinctive sexuality of the man is actualized in this relationship alone. Exactly for this reason, it is only one existential element among others. It lacks the indelible character that obtains in the case of the woman. On the whole therefore, the man's relationship to the woman—in spite of its decisive importance for his sexuality—does not possess that vital importance for him.

Evidently the typical situation is this: The fulfillment of sexual desire tends to free the man from the relationship and bind the woman to it. The external reasons for this are obvious. For the man, the motive that impelled him to the woman has disappeared with the satisfaction of the impulse. For the woman, on the other hand, the need for a protective relationship arises from pregnancy. Here as well, however, the general pattern is that for the man, the sexual question is a relational question. Thus it disappears completely as soon as he no longer has any interest in the relationship. His absolute is not bound up with his sexual being. For the woman, this is a question of her nature, which her absolute also secondarily translates into the relationship that proceeds from it. The man may be brought to madness or suicide as a result of erotic experiences. However, he feels that they are of no significance to what concerns him most deeply, insofar as we may be permitted to speak of matters that cannot be proved. Even in the expressions of erotic natures such as Michelangelo, Goethe, and Richard Wagner, there are enough imponderables that allude to this ranking of the erotic experience in their character.

For the man, the absolute that represents sexuality or eroticism as a cosmic principle becomes nothing more than the relationship to the woman. For the woman, the relativity that this domain possesses as a relationship between the sexes becomes the absolute, the autonomous being of her nature. On the one hand, the ultimate result of this constellation is the feeling, which is frequently confirmed, that even the most complete surrender of a woman does not release a final reserve of her soul. This is because she is *intrinsically* sexual, not merely in her relationship to the man. It is as if she has a secret sense of self-possession and a self-contained completeness. Since she offers herself quite completely, it is true that she includes this in the exchange. Even here, however, this secret self does not become accessible to the other person. On the contrary, although it has come to belong to him, it still always remains rooted in its own ground and inaccessibility.

In this context, the conceptualization of a matter that is really quite simple becomes difficult and easily confused. Insofar as the man translates his life and achievement into the form of objectivity—and thus beyond the dichotomous fact of sexuality—for him, sexuality consists only in a relationship. It exists *as* the relationship to women. For the woman, however, sexuality has become an absolute, an autonomous mode of being, inextricably bound up or identical with her ultimate essence in the fact of her femininity. This absolute merely acquires an expression, an empirical realization, in the relationship to the man. Within its own sphere, however, this relationship—precisely because it is the phenomenal expression of the fundamental being of the woman—is of absolutely incomparable significance for her.

This circumstance has led to the judgment—which in a deeper sense is completely false—that the definitive nature of the woman does not lie in herself but rather coincides with this relationship and is exhausted in it. Because there is a sense in which she already has the sexual life in itself, as the self-contained absolute of her nature, the woman does not so much need man in general. However, if this nature is to be expressed, her need for the man as an individual is all the more powerful. The man is much easier to arouse sexually because arousal is not an excitation of his total being but only of a partial function. Thus for him, only a quite general stimulus is necessary. As a result, we can understand that the woman is more dependent on the individual man, and the man more dependent on women in general.

On the basis of this fundamental structure, it becomes understandable, on the one hand, that a psychological instinct has always characterized the woman as the sexual being and, on the other hand, that women themselves frequently resist this characterization and feel that it is somehow mistaken. This is because we generally understand a sexual being—from the male standpoint—as primarily and fundamentally oriented to the other sex. Typically, however, this does not hold true for the woman. Her sexuality is so much an aspect of her immanent nature and it so unconditionally and directly constitutes her ultimate being that it is quite impossible for it to develop merely in the intentionality of her relationship to the man, or as this intentionality; nor could its nature be acquired in this way.

Perhaps this becomes most evident in the image of the old woman. The woman passes beyond the upper threshold of erotic attraction, in the active as well as the passive sense, at a much earlier age than the man. However, disregarding extremely rare exceptions and the deterioration of advanced old age, there is no sense in which this makes her masculine or, what is more to the point here, sexless. All her sexuality that is oriented to the man is extinguished. Neverthe-

less, the distinctively female quality of her total being remains unchanged. Everything in her that, until that point, seemed to derive its
purpose and meaning from her erotic relationship to the man is now
revealed as lying completely beyond this relationship, a self-
determined possession of her own nature with its own central focus.

This is why it seems to me that there is also no sense in which this
nature can be reduced to the relationship to a child instead of to the
relationship to a man. As is true of the man-woman relationship,
naturally, the immense significance of the mother-child relationship
for the woman is beyond question. As it is usually maintained,
however, it too provides nothing more than a definition from the
standpoint of the social interest, a modification of that other attitude
of the woman which shifts her into an instrumentally purposive
context that does not conform to her nature. At best, it is a projection
of her most distinctive and integral nature into the sequence of time
and into a heterogeneity that lies outside her.

If this end is posited, it immediately follows that women ultimately exist only for men. In the next generation, the female elements are eliminated as ultimate purposes. Again, they serve only as
instruments for the next succeeding generation, within which the
same process is repeated. Thus in every generation, only the male
elements remain as the purposes for the sake of which all this
transpires. Even this logical consistency shows that all such relations
are only *phenomenal expressions* of the metaphysical nature of the
woman to which its self-contained completeness and its immanence
cannot be reduced.

In its ultimate depths, of course, this nature remains utterly female. However, this femininity is not a phenomenon in the same
sense. It is not something relative, and thus it does not exist "for
another." In order to avoid misunderstandings, it should be noted
that this does not amount to egoism, because egoism always involves
a relationship to another person, a state of dissatisfaction with one's
own being, an interest in what lies outside the self and what one
would like to incorporate into his own existence. Although it conflicts with the popular view of the matter, this process of self-
instrumentalization, the abandonment of one's own center, approximates the most profound nature of the man much more closely than
that of the woman. Man creates the objective, or he implicates

himself in the objective, whether this be in the cognitive forms of representation or in the creative formation of given elements. Both his theoretical and his practical ideal include an element of depersonalization. He always discloses himself in a world that is in some way extensive, regardless of how much he may penetrate it with his personality. With his activity, he incorporates himself into historical orders within which he can constitute an instrument and a link, all of his power and sovereignty notwithstanding. In this respect, he is utterly different from the woman, whose existence is constructed on the basis of purely intensive presuppositions. In her periphery, perhaps she can be upset and destroyed more easily than the man. Nevertheless, regardless of how closely connected to the focal point of her existence this periphery may be—and the basic pattern of all female psychology seems to lie in the intimacy of this connection between the periphery and the centrality of existence—her existence rests in this unextended central point, withdrawn from all external orders.

Regardless of whether life is conceived as a subjectively internal orientation or by reference to its expression in things, the male individual always seems to be moved from two sides, within whose polarity the woman is not drawn. On the one hand, the man is charmed by the purely sensual (in contrast to the more profound female sexuality, which in general is less specifically sensual precisely because it is not so much a carnal matter). The will attracts him, the desire to absorb and dominate. On the other hand, he is also drawn to the spiritual, to absolute form and to the transcendent, which lies beyond desire. It is perhaps a fundamental error of Schopenhauer to misplace the vital significance of the latter in the mere negation of the former. The opposite error of Nietzsche is no less fundamental: to find nothing but the elemental will to power and life in every passion for the nonsensual and the trans-elemental. It seems to me that such a synthesis cannot be produced so easily. On the contrary, we shall probably have to rest content with the polarity (which as such is also a kind of unity) and the antithesis of these two inner tendencies as an ultimate fact. In contrast to this, the woman remains self-contained. Her world gravitates to its own distinctive center. Insofar as the woman lies beyond both of these tendencies— which are actually eccentric, that of sensual desire and transcendent form—she might even be described as the authentic "human being," as the being which is situated in the human in the most unqualified sense. The man, on the other hand, remains "half animal, half angel."

Consider now the turn to the object. On the one hand, it is a thoroughly male disposition to recognize the autonomous existence of things that follow their own laws as important and significant. The entire ideal of a kind of knowledge that is as objective and as pure as possible rests on this immanent presupposition. In addition, however, there is the interest in the formation and transformation of things, with the firm intent that they should exist and be constituted according to the dictates of the spirit.

As a type, the woman stands beyond this dual relationship to things. The idealism of pure theory, which signifies a relationship to that with which one has no relationship, is not her affair. If she does not feel that she is connected with something—either as regards its external or ethical-altruistic instrumental purposiveness, or as regards its significance for inner well-being—then it really does not concern her. It is as if she lacked what might be called the telegraphic connection which establishes the purely objectivistic interest. With respect to formation, on the other hand, male work—from that of the shoemaker and the carpenter to that of the painter and the poet—is the complete determination of objective form by means of subjective energy. But it is also the complete objectification of the subject. The woman may be completely and selflessly active, she may be quite fully productive and "creative" in her sphere, and she may have a thoroughly resolute ability to tune a home and even an entire area according to the timbre of her personality. Nevertheless productivity in the sense of the interpenetration and simultaneous autonomy of subject and object is not her concern. Knowledge and creation are dynamic relationships in which our existence is—as this might be put—drawn out of itself. They represent a displacement of the center, an annulment of that ultimate self-contained completeness of being which constitutes the meaning of life for the female type, even with all its external activity and its devotion to practical tasks. Consider the relationship to things the possession of which is in some way or other a general necessity. There is a sense in which the woman achieves this possession without leaving the existence in which she rests by means of a more immediate and instinctive—in a certain sense, a more naive—contact, or even identity, with things. Her form of existence is not a matter of that specific differentiation of subject and object that regains its synthesis only in the specific forms of knowledge and production.

Thus in spite of the development of his psychic contents in an absolute fashion, to which precisely this dualism disposes him, the man—thinking, producing, and socially active—is actually a much more relativistic being than the woman. Therefore his sexuality as well is developed only in the desire for a relationship, or the consummation of a relationship, with the woman. On the other hand, there is a sense in which the existence of the woman, which in its deepest signification is more undemanding (in spite of all the "wants" that characterize the more superficial levels of her existence), comprehends sexuality directly within itself. It is true that her metaphysical nature is directly fused with her existence as she experiences it. However, its immanent meaning should be completely differentiated from all her relationships and her existence as mediated by physiological, psychological, and social considerations. Almost all discussions about women represent only what they are in their real, ideal, or value relationship to men. No one asks what they are for themselves. Of course this is understandable enough: Male norms and requirements are not regarded as specifically male but rather as the objective and the generally valid itself. And because it is this relation alone which is considered from the outset, because the woman is regarded as subsisting essentially or exclusively in this *relationship*, the conclusion is drawn that for herself she is *nothing*, which only proves what is already taken for granted in the question.

On the other hand, consider the unconditional question of what the woman is for herself, or in an absolute sense. That question would either be falsely posed or falsely answered if her femininity were ignored. That is because femininity—and this is the single most crucial point—is not ascribed to her only on the basis of that relationship, as if she were a metaphysically colorless being. On the contrary, it constitutes her being in principle. It is an absolute that, unlike the male absolute, does not obtain above the sexual opposition but rather—with reservations that follow—beyond it.

So in the male nature there is a formal element that prepares the ground for its transcendence into an impersonal idea and norm that even lie beyond the real. Consider the grasp for what lies beyond himself in all his productive activities, the pervasive relationship to what is juxtaposed to him, to which the man devotes himself with his incorporation into extensive real and ideal sequences. From the outset, this comprises a dualism and a fragmentation of the unity of life into the forms of higher and lower, subject and object, the judge and the judged, means and end. Insofar as the female nature juxtaposes its fundamental—one might almost say immanently transcendent—unity to all these polar oppositions and superstructures and these distances between the subjective and the objective, the typical tragedy of each of the two sexes is revealed.

For the man, it lies in the relationship between finite achievement and infinite challenge. The challenge has two aspects. It comes from the self, insofar as the self only wants to transcend itself, to live creatively, and to prove itself. As regards the intention behind this act, there is no question of a limit. Nor is there any limitation from the side of the objective idea, which demands realization. In every work, the absoluteness of a consummation is ideally posited. When these two infinities clash, however, radical obstructions arise. Subjective energy, which from a purely immanent perspective is conscious neither of a limitation nor even of dimensions, reaches its limits in the moment that it turns itself toward the world and attempts to produce an object in it. This is because all production is possible only on the basis of a compromise with the forces of the world. It is a resultant of what we are and what the things themselves are. Even the pure mental entity exhibits the limitations imposed upon the intrinsically formless stream of spiritual energy by virtue of the necessities of logic, substance, and language. And the idea of the work itself is circumscribed and delimited because the work can be produced only by means of psychic energies the realization of which is necessarily finite.

This devaluation, disturbance, and destruction that affects all production is located in the presuppositions of production itself. The structure of soul and world, which is a condition for the possibility of all production, stamps it with the following contradiction: The immanent demand of its infinity is a priori linked with the immanent impossibility of fulfilling this demand. Insofar as it weighs upon every practically productive relationship between the person and the world, this is, of course, a general human tragedy. However, this tragedy develops only for the sex that produces this relationship out of its ultimate necessities, and for which life in the object, the given object and the object to be produced, arises out of its own fundamental basis.

In comparison with this profound inner necessity, the typical tragedy of the female develops out of her historical situation, or at least from the more external strata of her life. Here we do not find the dualism which splits the roots of existence and causes what might be called an indigenous tragedy. Life is lived and experienced as a value that rests in itself. As regards its meaning, it is so concentrated on its focal point that even the claim that life is an end in itself implies too much of a division. The entire category of means and ends, which is so deeply rooted in the masculine nature, simply does not apply on the same profound level to the feminine nature.

There is also the complication that, from the perspective of their temporal, social, and psychological destinies, these beings are treated and valued as mere instruments. Moreover, they even develop this consciousness of themselves: as an instrument for the man, the home, the child. Perhaps this should be called pathos rather than tragedy. This is because tragedy exists only under the following condition: In spite of the fact that a destructive fate is directed against the subject's will to live, it still has its origin in an ultimate attitude of this subject and the depths of this very will to live. Purely external forces, on the other hand—regardless of how terrifying, tormenting, or destructive they may be—can produce a fate that is wretched in the extreme, but never one that is tragic in the authentic sense.

However, the case of women is quite distinctive. That transcendence of herself, that abandonment of the profound fusion of her life in order to enter a more extended sequence and to serve it and its other elements, cannot be represented simply as an external violation of her nature. It is, of course, situated not in the metaphysical meaning of the life of woman, but rather in the fact that she stands in a world that is replete with "the other." To have a relationship with this world inevitably shatters the state of pure repose in the inner center. The dualism which is responsible for the typical tragedy of femininity springs not from the deepest and most intrinsic properties of the woman's being, as in the case of the man, but rather from the transposition of being into the natural and historical world.

Perhaps this could also be expressed by saying that what could be called the natural tragedy is only grounded in the being of the male. (Assuming that the following somewhat vague expressions are allowed, the natural is too much a part of the metaphysical ground of the woman's substance to develop a tragic dualism here.) Regardless of the extent to which a man may live and die for an idea, he always juxtaposes himself to it. For him, the idea is an infinite task, and in the ideal sense, he always remains the solitary individual. Since this juxtaposition and opposition represent the only form in which the man can conceive and experience an idea, it seems to him as if women were "incapable of having any ideas" (Goethe). For the woman, however, her existence and the idea are one and the same. In spite of a fateful isolation that may occasionally master her, typically she is never as solitary as the man. She is always at home with herself. However, the man has his "home" beyond himself.

This is why men in general become bored more easily than women. For men, the process of life and the sense in which its content has value are not so organically and self-evidently interrelated as is the case for women. Women are more protected from boredom than men by the continuity of the more or less large and small tasks posed by domestic life. This is only the external historical realization of a profoundly different quality of existence. As regards both its quality and its dimensions, the process of life as such has a meaning for women—and this is connected with the metaphysical significance of the natural for women—that is obviously quite different from its meaning for men. Moreover, it is a significance that includes the "idea" in a special sense. Anatomists have established that women, even at the peak of their physical development, resemble children more closely than men do—in the proportions of the skeletal frame, the relative composition of fat tissue and musculature, and the formation of the larynx. This analogy is not limited to the constitution of the body. It was the occasion for Schopenhauer's obvious—but not inevitable—conclusion that women remain "overgrown children for their entire lives."

As regards psychic existence (including the areas where it borders on physical existence), it is characteristic of youth to experience life above all as life itself, as a process and a homogeneous stream of reality. Youth wants to unfold the bound-up energies of life simply because they are there and are disposed in this direction. In this respect, youth differs from age, in which the contents of life become increasingly more important than its process. Concerning women, we might say that there is a sense in which they live more, they must have a more concentrated and readily accessible life, than men. This is because the woman's life must also suffice for the child. However, this does not yet involve a greater amount of residual and externally visible energy.

Consider the vital significance of the process of life, what might be described as the penetration into the depths of life as such, that we experience in the typical woman. It produces the result that the idea, the abstract and normatively expressible content of life which is ideally differentiated from life itself, does not develop itself in and for women with a comparable autonomy and completeness. In light of the entire meaning of the woman's existence and her existential form, it also holds true that the idea is simply not destined for such an autonomous existence in her. Moreover, this notion that the woman acquires her significance from her life process and not from its results is still not entirely satisfactory.

If we want to express the matter quite precisely, for women, it is not a question of the distinction between process and result or idea, as it is for youth. For women it is rather a question of life in a sense that is so homogeneous that it cannot be distinguished into form and process. Here life and the idea have the relationship of immediacy, from which the value of an inner world—or a world of inner values as well—is constructed, just as this is possible for men in the form of the separation of life from the idea. The "logical deficiency" that in general is implicitly ascribed to women must be related to this. Regardless of the extent to which this reproach may be both superficial and mistaken, its universality alludes to some sort of factual basis from which it develops.

In the domain of knowledge, logic represents—in relation to the immediacy of vital, psychic reality—the most complete differentiation and independence imaginable of the normative and the ideal. Whoever regards himself as bound by logic sees himself to a certain extent as confronted by the domain of truth, which demands con-

formity from his actual thought. Even if our thought completely
diverges from the domain of truth, there is no sense in which it
forfeits its inner validity or its claim on our mental processes. As a
result of this quality of logical norms, the idea and the reality of our
thought are placed in absolute opposition. The latter does not satisfy
the demand imposed on it directly and automatically. The former
exercises no unquestionable real power.

However, such a dualism conflicts with the female principle.
Conceived abstractly, this principle comes into play at the point
where the reality of the expressions of our existence and the idea or
norm have not diverged. It does not lie in a compound of the two,
but rather in a continuous unity which is a thoroughly self-conscious
entity and exists with the same legitimacy as each of the sequences
that are developed separately by the male spirit. The conclusion that
is drawn from these complete oppositions—namely, that they rule
out a direct uniformity on conceptual grounds—holds true only for
the level of sequences that is already formed for divergence. In this
context, however, the question concerns a distinctive inner state in
which this divergence does not take place. In any case, this is the
regulative principle that produces the differential orientation of the
female nature, regardless of whether there is a more or less conscious
sense of the distance between logic and psychic reality in individual
phenomena.

This is why the male endeavor to unify existence and idea in the
most diverse substantive areas is often unintelligible to the woman.
In many cases, she possesses directly what for the man is the result of
abstraction: in other words, a result of the reconstitution of what was
formerly divided. In these cases, what we call the female instinct—
regardless of how it is psychologically analyzed in detail—is only this
unmediated unity of the psychic process with the norms and criteria
which are differentiated from it, and which provide the basis for the
validity that is ascribed to it.

Perhaps there is an instinct that has its origins in the collective
experiences of the species and their transmission through the physical media of inheritance. But there is another instinct as well that is
prior to all experience. In this instinct, the psychic elements, which
must have already been distinguished in order to constitute experience, exist in an undifferentiated unity. The truth content of these

elements is due to the mysterious relation—which will occupy us shortly—that seems to obtain between this profound unity of total psychic existence and that of the cosmos in general. In the first form of this instinct, the elements that constitute experience have once again come together in a psychic unity. In the other form, these elements remain undifferentiated. In both cases, the light of consciousness which these elements (Kant called them sentience and understanding) acquire as a result of separation and conflict is missing.

Although genuine genius rarely occurs among women, it has frequently been noted that genius has something of the feminine about it. This remarkable phenomenon clearly does not pertain merely to the production of the work, whose unconscious ripening, nourished by the total being of the personality, is analogous to the growth of the child in the mother. On the contrary, it is the a priori unity of life and the idea, on which the female nature rests. The genius repeats this unity on the highest level, where the object is produced. Thus consider the obscurity of that metaphysical relationship, the earlier form of the instinct which the conscious procedure of logic endeavors to replace, correct, and secure. Under these circumstances, it is understandable that the female instinct and unmediated female knowledge can be just as frequently in error as correct.

So there is no sense in which the so-called logical deficiency is a simple defect. On the contrary, it is only the negative expression of the quite positively determined female mode of being. This very mode of being is repeated in another phenomenon which translates that logical deficiency into another dimension. It is said that women are not fond of offering "proofs." Logic and proof rest on that tension between the real process of our thought and objective truth, the validity of which is independent of this process and the attainment of which is the aim of thought. As I indicated, the duality of this relationship is expressed in logic: the fact that in all of our actual thought we know we are bound by a norm which does not belong to this reality but rather to an autonomous realm of truth. In proof, the other feature comes to the fore: the *indirection*, which in countless cases is the only basis on which our actual thought process can arrive at self-sufficient truth. Purely intellectual movement tends to achieve a correspondence with its object not at the moment of its inception but only at the end of a path that is more or less replete with stations. The character of a path or of mediacy is a primary fact of our intellectuality. Not every proof is an indirect proof, but all proof is an indirect entity. Moreover, all proof—regardless of whether it is brief and simple or based on a long chain of premises—proceeds in such a way that something novel and provisionally problematic is derived from something that is firmly established and already acknowledged. The ultimate datum cannot be proven. That is because its proof would mean that it is not ultimate but rather based on something that is still more fundamental.

This immutable form of all proof is responsible for its incompatibility with the female existence in its depth and its metaphysical relationship to existence in general, because—regardless of whether this is defensible or reasonable in individual cases—female existence is directly grounded in the fundamental as such. The woman perceives the primary and unprovable element in every *thema probandum*. There is a sense in which she does not need and cannot use the roundabout method of proof. The general submersion of the female type in existence allows her instinct to speak out, as if from an existential unity with objects that requires no mediation. It is as if her knowledge resided—and resided exclusively—in that ultimate datum on which all proofs are based and in which they rest, as if *in nuce*. As a result, the form of method that is characteristic of all our discursive knowledge is unnecessary and irrelevant for her.

Thus consider all the inadequacies of knowledge that are a consequence of this matter—for there are countless occasions on which the problems of inquiry can be solved only discursively and not in the coincidence of the beginning point and the end. The entire fact, so frequently criticized, that women do not like to undertake proofs and do not want to have something proven is not an isolated deficiency, but is rooted in the fundamental mode of her type of being and its relationship to existence in general. It will become increasingly clear that the authentic definition of the female nature, in its metapsychological sense, is the following: The purely immanent significance of its subjective structure which does not extend beyond the limits of the psyche possesses, as such and immediately, a metaphysical connection or unity with existence in general, with something that we are obliged to call the ground of things.

This stands in the most profound contrast to the male nature. The true, the being of the cosmos, and the norm do not yet reside in the immediate and immanent psychic reality of the man's nature. On the contrary, from the standpoint of its own structure, the man's nature sees itself as *juxtaposed* to all this, as something to be accomplished or something that cannot be accomplished, as an imperative or an intellectual task. The spiritual expression of this nature is logic, which rests on the dualism between the real psychological world and the ideal world of truth that it does not touch, and proof, which presupposes the discursive character of knowledge and the necessity of method and of the roundabout method.

Insofar as the woman—with that inner unity that transcends the need for logic—is somehow immediately situated in the things themselves, in the truth and above reality, she is indifferent to proof, which is only supposed to lead us to this reality in the form of method. The one refusal exhibits the immanent formation, the other refusal the transcendent formation, of the female nature. This formation can be grasped in an extremely schematic and epigrammatic fashion, and in opposition to masculinity as such, in the thesis that its transcendence lies precisely in its immanence.

This distinctiveness of the woman, independent of any relationship to the masculine, is most complete and significant in the ethical domain. Here the dualism of reality and the idea clashes so forcefully, and the entire sphere of the ethical seems to be so exclusively erected upon this abyss as if on its own foundation, that it seems as if the form of the male nature alone would correspond to the depth and seriousness of the problems. This is why a thinker such as Weininger, who is thoroughly committed to an extreme male dualism and the unabashed conflation of the male and the human ideal, begins precisely at the point of the ethical in order to prove the absolute value nullity of the female nature on this basis. Moreover, he undertakes this in a thoroughly logical fashion, so that this nature seems to him to be not evil or immoral but rather simply amoral, detached from the ethical problem in general.

The phenomenon called the beautiful soul shows that the moral possibility of life is not based exclusively on the dualism between the moral imperative and the real natural impulse. It is characteristic of the beautiful soul that its moral conduct does not depend upon surmounting opposing motives. On the contrary, it stems from the self-evidence of an impulse in which there is no conflict. For the beautiful soul, there is a sense in which life is unilinear: From the outset, it wants only what it should.

In this context, everything depends upon the fundamental possibility that the metaphysical unity of nature in us and the idea above us is disclosed as the inner harmony of our volitional actions. There are two paths to this disclosure, which can be called the transdualistic or male and the predualistic or female. On the other hand, it can be attained by the gradual refinement and tranformation of a nature whose impulses are originally opposed to those of morality and for whom duty is an onerous imperative. Each act of self-conquest makes the next easier, and the continual and successful struggle against the unethical permanently weakens it. As a result, even impulses that are immediately natural develop in the direction of the ethical. Wherever this transformation is complete, the original dualism has become the unity of the beautiful soul. The other form of the beautiful soul, however, does not need to surmount a dualism. On the contrary, it possesses unity as an immediate and immanent principle. Its unity can bear the idea within itself, not merely as the prize of the struggle and the oppositions that have been overcome but rather as the a priori unbroken life of the will itself. These two forms correspond exactly to the two forms of the instinct for theoretical validity noted above. One gradually succeeds in establishing a relationship between disparate elements. The other is a unit of precisely these elements; it obtains prior to any separation, and thus it requires no relationship.

Here we find the ethical type which—realized from every aspect, male as well as female—is most profoundly linked with the basic female nature and develops most directly out of its existential mold. Consider that profound immanence and autonomy of women which we always feel, that life which develops from a more homogeneous basis than the man's. In what follows we shall discuss how its ultimate significance lies in the presentiment or the metaphysical truth of the following consideration: This integral and distinctive existence is also more than women's own existence; in the depths of their submersion into themselves, women are at one with the basis of life itself.

At this juncture, the same point that was expressed earlier from the standpoint of existence is now made from the standpoint of the norm. Suppose we describe the specifically male dualism in a quite one-sided fashion, as situated "between sensual happiness and the peace of the soul." What is most characteristic of the female nature replaces this male dualism—regardless of how frequently psychological and historical complications implicate the feminine nature in this dualsim—with a unified, inner orientation.

In the first place, this subjective unity—within the currents of the psyche, it predominates purely as such—is observed infinitely more often, and also more fundamentally, in women than in men. Moreover, women themselves are more conscious of it than men are. It is a state in which one has come to terms with oneself; a mode of conduct that is not intrinsically disturbed by its own counter-instances, comparable to the manner in which a plant puts forth branches and fruit; an imperative mode of being and acting that is still aware of its own unconstrained freedom because, of their own accord, all the currents of its nature flow in one direction.

In this context, the following point is decisive: This immanent unity which is consummated within the subjective life is also experienced as a unity with the moral idea, with what this idea requires from the subject. Consider what the dualistic ethic proclaims as the inferiority of women: that they behave naively and on the whole enjoy a better conscience than men. That is a consequence of this undifferentiated status of existence and norm in women. Of course the inner continuity of the practical nature need not always realize the idea that has moral value, no more than this holds true for the dualistic male mode. There is a sense in which it exhibits only the form, but not always the content, of the beautiful soul. However, suppose that a specifically female type of the ethical exists. (Given the psychic transitions between the poles of the male and the female, there is no sense in which this holds true for the morality of all female individuals.) In that case, it stems from that unity of existence which is its unity with the idea. In light of these considerations, perhaps the following can be claimed concerning the quality of morality that is distinctive for the female existential character: For women, it is subjectively more secure but objectively more hazardous than for men.

All the foregoing considerations are only intended to demonstrate the profound submersion of the woman—rejecting everything external to her—into her own existence, an absolute female existence. Here again, the independence of the female existence is exhibited vis-à-vis the mere relationship to the man, from which her existence allegedly acquires its nature. At the same time, this consideration shows why femininity, in spite of its immanent absolute status, must relinquish to the male principle the establishment of the trans-sexually objective world—theoretical as well as normative—that is juxtaposed to the self. In order to avert any suspicion that this implies the denigration of women to a declassé status, we should emphasize that, in principle, quite the same *contents* of spirit and life can be realized in both the male and the female *form*. In this respect, they only fall under a different a priori for their synthesis. Moreover, consider the fundamental, even absolute, unity of the woman's being with her sexual existence. It is responsible for the fact that sexuality in the usual male, relational sense has a secondary status for her. This holds true regardless of how immensely important the relationship may become for her as a phenomenon of that absolute, which almost completely incorporates her into itself.

This basic fact has the result that none of the expressions of women, none of the phenomena and objectivations of her nature, is perceived as generally human. On the contrary, in relation to the expressions of the nature of the male, which are perceived as trans-sexual and purely objective, they are collectively perceived as specifically female. Man lacks the orientation to a *specific* external entity that is given to the woman by virtue of the unity of her existence with her existence as woman. This is why a quite profound intention oriented to the general—and thus to the trans-subjectively objective as well—lies in the male. Consider all historical power relations which have given these products the prerogative of objective determinants, dominating the opposition between the sexes in an objectively absolute fashion because this opposition is irrelevant to them. They only project into temporal orders the inner characterological difference which the relationship of the sexual moment exhibits for the totality of being in men and women.

There is a sense in which this is logically expressed in the fact that the male nature is much more difficult to determine and define than the female. The generally human, of which sexual specificity should be a special case, is congruent with the masculine in the respect that no specific difference from the masculine can be identified in the generally human. The general as such cannot be defined. Yet suppose that certain features are cited as distinctively male. A closer examination establishes that these features are always intended only as differences from specifically female features. However, the nature of the latter features is not identified in an analogous fashion, purely on the basis of an opposition to the masculine. They are perceived, rather, more as an intrinsically exisiting and intrinsically defined entity, as a distinctive type of humanity which, however, is in no sense fixed exclusively by means of an opposition. Consider the old idea which extends from the level of brutal and ignorant self-aggrandizement to that of the most sublime philosophical speculation: that only the male is the genuine human. This idea finds its conceptual pendant in the greater facility with which the nature of the woman, compared with that of the man, is defined. For this reason, there are innumerable psychologies of women, but hardly one psychology of men.

This most profound source of difference between the sexes is also documented in a superficial psychological phenomenon: In general, the average man's interest in women lies in something that is roughly the same in both the seamstress and the princess. It is easy to understand that this relationship in the possibilities of definition is reversed as soon as individuals, rather than the sexual type, are at stake: On the whole, we can describe the individual man better than the individual woman. This is not only a consequence of the fact that, because of the social predominance of the man, the entire linguistic conceptualization of our culture corresponds to the male coloration of mental processes. It is true that the genus woman is important enough to require concepts of definition. However, the universe of language has not concerned itself with the individualized characteristics of women, and the fine nuances that are essential here are just as often unavailable for the psychological description of individual women as they are for women themselves in their attempt to make themselves fully understandable to men.

Another relationship is more basic. The individual woman is more difficult to define than the individual man because she is easier to define as a genus. Suppose that the general concept is aleady perceived as something that is specific and differentially defined. In that case, there is a sense in which individualization is incorporated into the general and exhausts itself in it. As a result, there is actually no more space for the further process of individualization and no more interest in it. This is why the phenomena of a most profound feature of the woman's nature belong in this context: It holds true for the woman much more than for the man that the general lives in the form of the personally individual. In the typically complete woman, much that is quite generic and actually impersonal becomes something completely personal. It is produced in a thoroughly inward fashion, as if it made its entry into the world from the unique point of the personality here and for the first time. Of course there is nothing more general than erotic relationships. And whereas there are countless occasions on which the man also experiences them and treats them in this way, they seem to constitute the specifically personal fate of the woman, not a generic event that happens to her, but rather her inherently most characteristic productivity. This also holds true for her relationship to the child, both before and after its birth—this most typical of all relationships, which extends so deeply into the subhuman. For the woman, however, this takes place in the most basic depths of her soul. This relationship, which is so completely impersonal that it is nothing more than a transitional point in the development of the species, grows out of the center in which all the energies of her nature coalesce to form her personality.

Finally, morality—which is nothing more than the form of life of the social sphere, the conduct that it has stamped with the form of a law in order to ensure its own preservation—seems to stem from the innermost instinct of woman's nature. She "aspires to morality," which is often an obstacle to the mobility of the male. However, it fits the nature of the woman like her skin. Within the domain of morality, she finds the freedom that, for the man, lies overwhelmingly outside it (granting all the individual exceptions to this typical and historical phenomenon). This is because freedom means that the law of our conduct is the expression of our own nature. On the basis of these embodiments of the general in the personal, it is perfectly understandable that although this being can be typologically defined, its personal aspect as such easily resists definition.

Suppose, on the other hand, that the general aspect of a being is as thoroughly general as holds true in the case of the man, so that his specifically male character as such becomes the historical synonym for human universality. In that case, the definition of his specificity as that of an individual can be developed more readily and precisely. There is more room available for such a definition. Thus it is easier to define the female than the male, but more difficult to define a woman than a man. This matter has also disclosed itself as an expression of the fundamental configuration which situates this case within an infinitely more comprehensive type of human spirituality and metaphysics: From the relativity or interdefinability in which the male and the female nature is exhibited, the male nature arrogates to itself the category of the absolute, and thus dominates the entire relativity of which it is also a part.

I have previously pointed out that this absolute emphasis upon one side of a correlation over and above the totality of its two sides usually does not remain confined to this side. On the contrary, it generally happens that different partitions sometimes endow one side with the accent of the absolute, and sometimes the other side. The distinctive posture of the spirit in relation to the contents of the world is characterized by the fact that there is some sense in which every absolute is conceived relatively. In other words, its nature is defined by reference to its relationship with another entity. However, everything relative can transcend its relation into an autonomous and absolute existence. In view of all the foregoing considerations, therefore, not only the male principle but also the female occupies a position beyond the relativity that, on first glance, is responsible for the meaning of both. The female principle takes this position not only for the reason indicated in the foregoing sketch: because of its indifference to the male principle and its relationship to this existence, but also in a positive transcendence of the male complex of differentiation, which embraces both the male and the female. The man stands above the opposition of sexuality to the extent that even objective norms themselves are male. (Although this often seems to be nothing more than a historical violation, in its essence, it is prefigured in the structure of the male spirit.) The woman, on the other hand, stands beyond this opposition because, in her existence, she lives directly at and by means of the source from which both sides of this opposition flow.

In the same way that the man, independent of this relationship, is more than male, so the woman is more than female. This is because she represents the universal fundament that comprehends the sexes substantially or genetically. It is because she is the mother. In the former case, the absolute arises as the trans-sexually objective, which is male. In the latter case, it arises as the trans-sexually fundamental, which is female. In the former case, action and development exhibit the dualism in whose form the human being transcends itself, and which is specifically male. So in the latter case, existence exhibits the unity in whose form the human being, in a certain sense, penetrates beneath itself into the undifferentiated possibility of all developments. This existence is not, of course, colorless but rather female. However, its ultimate essence detaches itself from every relation that could define it by reference to the antithesis of masculinity. This makes it possible to experience the feminine—whose first and unmediated expression is motherhood—as an absolute, on which both the masculine and the feminine in the relational sense are preeminently based.

At this point, a metaphysical presupposition comes to the fore. Although it is remote from any possibility of proof, it moves throughout the whole of intellectual history as a presentiment, an impression, and a speculation: the idea that the more deeply a person becomes absorbed in his own being and the more clearly he allows this to be expressed in himself, the closer he comes to the existence and the unity of the cosmos as such, and the more completely he brings this unity to expression in himself. It is not only the mysticism of all ages that lives by this conviction. It also comes into play— explicitly and implicitly, and in the most manifold variations imaginable—in the much clearer world views of Kant and Schleiermacher, Goethe and Schopenhauer, which are so diametrically opposed to one another. The distinctively mystical feeling by means of which the typical attitude toward women has always been characterized may have a basis that can be expressed in the obscure awareness that these beings are more completely and integrally situated in their existence than men are; that all the turbulence of action and development, in the opposition of things as well as in the opposition of life itself, has less bearing on the substantial ground of their existence and absorbs it to a more limited extent; that ultimately, they remain more profoundly and immovably entrenched in their own nature; and that for them, the ground of existence as such, the obscure and inscrutable unity of life and the world, is their own ultimate ground, precisely by this means and to just this extent. As regards her most authentic nature, the woman lives on the basis of her own ground more than the man—insofar as her nature is not deflected by the violations and displacements of history and by influences which affect her as result of the *relationship* between the sexes.

This would have no significance unless there were some sense in which that ground were also the ground of things. The connection between the two lies in motherliness. However, this only exhibits an ultimate metaphysical unity in the form of temporality and life as bound to matter. And if we introduce the more psychological or, if one will, the more formal concept of the immanent completeness of existence, this is only a way of giving a different contour to the same content.

On the basis of the dualism of his nature, the man no doubt generally experiences the woman—regardless of how frequently he himself, culture, and fate implicate her as well into such a dualism— as a being that is inherently more complete than he is; in other words, as a being whose single essential aspects are not antagonistic to one another. On the contrary, the essential unity that holds between all these single aspects and cannot be designated in any other way is expressed as an immediately intimate and associative relationship. The remarkable aspect of this lies in the consideration that it is precisely the self-contained completeness of an intrinsic mode of existence that comprises a most forceful, symbolic, or metaphysical directive to the cosmic totality that lies outside it, or of which it is an element.

By means of its frame, the work of art, in its impenetrable, circumscribed limits, separates itself from the heterogeneous confusion of things. It becomes a symbol of existence in general in precisely this fashion. In a similar way and in comparison with the man, the woman represents a unity that is implicated in the multitude of the splintered fragments of life. It is not only the externals of morality that have always prohibited her from engaging in impetuosity, aggressive language, and ruthless self-assertion. On the contrary, consider the fact that this avoidance of all centrifugal and sweeping expansive gestures, this inner cohesiveness of her entire existence, became the form of her morality. This is the historical expression of that *self-contained completeness of her nature* which constitutes the more profound and general basis of all individual psychological states. That is why this form of existence is responsible for the relationship of the feminine nature to the totality of existence, a relationship that is obscurely felt and provides the occasion for the most curious reactions.

Although a part of the totality of the cosmos, the work of art exists as a counterpart to the cosmos by virtue of its self-contained completeness. It thereby alludes to an inexpressible metaphysical entity on which this equivalence of form is based. In the same way, it is the self-contained completeness of the form of the female nature that has always lent an air of cosmic symbolism to the woman. It is as if she had a relationship to the ground and totality of things in general that lies beyond all tangible particulars. Beside all the scorn and maltreatment of women, the feeling has broken forth throughout the entire history of culture, from primitive times on, that they were still something other than mere women: that is, other than beings that exist merely in their relationship to men. Since this is, of course, true, it seemed to follow that they had relationships to mysterious powers as prophetesses and witches, beings from which either a blessing or a curse appeared from the otherwise inaccessible womb of things, and thus beings that had to be either mystically revered, prudently avoided, or cursed as demons.

None of these vulgarities or flights of the poetic imagination has any sort of single characteristic or activity as its ultimate basis. Although there is no doubt that they all can be traced back to a unified motive of the utmost profundity, it will not be possible to identify such a uniquely specifiable motive historically. On the contrary, it seems that their basis lies in the following consideration. A nature that is so profoundly grounded in its own undifferentiated existence and which hardly emerges from itself at all was experienced as having a special proximity, as in a kind of relationship of identity, to being as such, regardless of whether this is called the ultimate ground of nature, the supernaturally mystical, or the metaphysical in the strict sense. The special sense in which the woman is absolute submerges her in the unity of existence. The absolute character of the man, on the other hand, pulls him away from existence to the idea.

In light of our existing modes of thought—regardless of how asymptotically or symbolically they may be related to reality—we are obliged to ground the many-faceted, the dynamic, and the one-sided by means of what might be called a static unity. In the case of the male nature, there is a sense in which this unity is absorbed by those dualistic and differentiated forms of life and expressions. In the case of the female nature, however, it continues to exist as her palpable substance, as if the motherhood of every woman repeated the process that differentiates and highlights the one-sided and dynamic quality of the individual entity from the obscure and diffuse ground of existence.

Thus it can be said that the more completely and profoundly a woman is female in this absolute sense, the less she is a woman in the relative sense, with reference to her differential relationship to the man. The same relationship, which can only be expressed as a paradox, also holds true for the man. Suppose it is his specifically male characteristic to build the world of the objective and the normative above what might be called the unilinear and subjective life, a world from the perspective of which the entire male-female dichotomy is something that is, in principle, arbitrary. In that case, he is less a man in the sense of this sexual relativity the more he is a man in the sense of that quite distinctively male achievement whose goal is the absolute.

One of the meanings of the "general" comes into play in the most profound character of each of the sexes: the general as the abstract that lies beind the individual phenomena; and the general as the substantial unity that is prior to individual phenomena. I am not at all inclined to confine the profusion of life within the limits of a symmetrical system. However, suppose we want to obtain the anatomical structure for the picture of animate reality that is our aim here (for it is skeletons that exhibit precisely that schematic symmetry, and it is only physiological processes that raise them into the play of life, which is infinitely complex and can no longer be grasped by means of a simple comparison). In that case, it seems that this dual absolute circumscribes the relationship between the sexes on the basis of which they mutually maintain their distinctive character. On the one hand, there is the masculine as the absolute. It is more than masculine, and it signifies objectivity, which, at the price of dualism, reaches the normative summit that transcends all subjectivity and all conflict. On the other hand, there is the feminine as the absolute on which the unity of human nature rests in a substantial and static self-contained completeness, in a sense prior to the division into subject and object.

FLIRTATION

Plato's wisdom concerning love—that it is an intermediate state between having and not-having—does not seem to touch the profundity of love's nature but only one form of its manifestation. It is not merely that his definition leaves no room for the love that says, "If I love you, what does that have to do with you?" Actually, it can refer only to the kind of love that expires with the fulfillment of its yearning. If love lies on the path from not-having to having, if its nature is exhausted in the movement to having, then when it "has," it can no longer be the same as it was before. It can no longer be love. On the contrary, its energy quantum is transformed into pleasure, or perhaps into lassitude.

This consequence of love—the yearning of one who lacks something for what he does not have—is not nullified by the consideration that love may arise anew in the very moment of its passing. From the perspective of its meaning, love remains fixed within a process of rhythmic oscillation. The moments of fulfillment lie in its pauses. However, where love is anchored in the ultimate depths of the soul, the cycle of having and not-having describes only the shape of its expression and its outward aspect. The being of love, the pure phenomenon of which is desire, cannot be terminated by the appeasement of this desire.

Regardless of whether the desire for possession signifies the definitive quality of love or only the swelling of the rhythm of the waves that play above this quality, where the object of love is a woman and its subject a man, it rises above the characteristic psychic fact of "pleasure." Pleasure is the source from which having and not-having are fed when they acquire for us the status of delight or torment, desire or apprehension. Here as elsewhere, however, there is a reversal of the connection between a possession and its valuation. Importance and value do not merely augment the possession and nonpossession of the object that pleases us; when possession and nonpossession acquire significance and weight for us, on whatever basis, their object tends to excite our pleasure as well. Thus it is not only the attractiveness of a commodity that determines the price we are willing to pay for it. There are, rather, countless occasions on which the item is attractive and desirable to us only because it costs something. Its production is not a matter to be taken for granted but rather one that requires sacrifice and effort. The possibility of this psychological turn is responsible for the development of the relationship between men and women into the form of flirtation.

In itself, the fact that the flirt "wants to please" does not account for her behavior. To define flirtation as simply a "passion for pleasing" is to confuse the means to an end with the desire for this end. A woman may exert herself in order to please in every way possible, from exercising the most subtle spiritual charms to the most audacious display of her physical attractions. In spite of all this, she can still be quite different from the flirt. This is because the distinctiveness of the flirt lies in the fact that she awakens delight and desire by means of a unique antithesis and synthesis: through the alternation or simultaneity of accommodation and denial; by a symbolic, allusive assent and dissent, acting "as if from a remote distance"; or, platonically expressed, through placing having and not-having in a state of polar tension even as she seems to make them felt concurrently. In the behavior of the flirt, the man feels the proximity and interpenetration of the ability and the inability to acquire something. This is the essence of "price." With that twist that turns value into the epigone of price, flirtation makes this acquisition seem valuable and desirable. The essence of flirtation, expressed with paradoxical brevity, is this: Where love is present, having and not-having are also present, whether in its fundament or in its external aspect. And thus where having and not-having are present—even if not in reality but only in play—love, or something that fills its place, is also present.

I shall apply this interpretation of flirtation first to some observations of experience. A sidelong glance with the head half-turned is characteristic of flirtation in its most banal guise. A hint of aversion lies in this gesture; but at the same time it connotes fleeting submission, a momentary focusing of attention on the other person, who in the same moment is symbolically rebuffed by the inclination of the body and the head. Physiologically, this glance cannot last longer than a few seconds, so that the withdrawal of the glance is already prefigured as something unavoidable in the glance itself. It has the charm of secrecy and furtiveness that cannot persist, and for this reason consent and refusal are inseparably combined in it.

The full face-to-face glance, no matter how penetrating and compelling it may be, never has this distinctive quality of flirtation. The swinging and swaying movement of the hips, the "strutting" walk, lies in the same category of flirtatious effects. It is not merely because this gait palpably stresses these effects through the motion of the parts of the body that generate sexual excitement, even though distance and reserve are in fact maintained at the same time, but rather because it incarnates concession and withdrawal in the playful rhythm of constant alternation. If flirtation extends beyond the movements and the expression of its own subject, that is only a technical modification of this simultaneity of implicit consent and refusal. Flirtation is fond of utilizing what might be called extraneous objects: dogs, flowers, children. On the one hand, this diverts attention away from the person for whom the flirtation is intended. On the other hand, this very diversion makes it clear to him how enviable the apparent object is. It is a way of saying: "It is not you that interests me, but rather these things here." And yet at the same time: "This is a game I'm playing for your benefit. It is because of my interest in you that I turn to these other things."

If we want to fix the polar coordinates of flirtation conceptually, it exhibits three possible syntheses. Flirtation as flattery: "Although you might indeed be able to conquer me, I won't allow myself to be conquered." Flirtation as contempt: "Although I would actually allow myself to be conquered, you aren't able to do it." Flirtation as provocation: "Perhaps you can conquer me, perhaps not—try it!" This movement between having and not-having—or, rather, this symbolic interpenetration of the two—clearly expresses the woman's focus of her attention on a man different from the one she really has in mind. This is not so brutally simple a matter as jealousy. Jealousy has a different locus, and when it is unconditionally provoked in order to intensify the desire for either acquisition or possession into a passion, it no longer falls in the category of flirtation. On the contrary, flirtation must make the person for whom it is intended feel the variable interplay between consent and refusal; the unwillingness to submit oneself that could be an indirect way to self-surrender; the surrender of the self behind which the withdrawal of the self stands as a background, a possibility, and a threat. Every conclusive decision brings flirtation to an end. The sovereign peak of its art is exhibited in its apparent approximation to a definitive condition, while at every moment balancing this condition by its opposite. When a woman flirts "with" one man in order to flirt with another who is the actual object of her intentions, the double meaning of the word "with" is profoundly revealed. On the one hand, it refers to an instrument; on the other hand, to the member of a correlation, as if we could not make a person into a mere means without this functioning in a reciprocal and retroactive fashion as well.

Finally, a certain fact—whose primary significance is physical, even though it has a psychic significance as well—perhaps demonstrates the most direct coincidence of consent and refusal, which have equally legitimate places in the coloration of flirtation: the fact of "semi-concealment." Under this heading I understand all those internal and external cases in which submission or presentation of the self is suspended by partial concealment or refusal of the self, in such a way that the whole is fantasized all the more vividly and the desire for the totality of reality is excited all the more consciously and intensively, as a result of the tension between this form and that of reality as incompletely disclosed.

It is remarkable how the historical development of the concealment of the body demonstrates this motive of simultaneous presentation and refusal. In contemporary ethnography, it is regarded as certain that the covering of the sexual organs, and clothing in general, originally had nothing at all to do with the feeling of shame. Rather, it served only the need for ornamentation and the closely related intention of exercising sexual attraction by means of concealment. Among peoples who go naked, there are cases in which only prostitutes wear clothing! The girdles and petticoats that fulfill the function of a fig leaf are often quite minimal and designed in such a way that concealment as such simply cannot be their purpose at all. They must have another purpose. Another phenomenon shows what this purpose is: In an extraordinary number of cases, they are quite garishly colored and ornamented in the most striking fashion. Thus their purpose is clearly to draw attention to these parts of the body. Originally, therefore, this concealment is only ornamental, with the dual function of all ornament: first, only to make the ornamented entity more *noticeable;* and then to make this entity appear valuable and attractive, to appear eminently *worthy of attention,* as well.

However, this ornament, like the ornamentation of the body in general, can fulfill this function only insofar as it also conceals. Because of this coincidence, the moment of flirtation is given with the primitive form of attire: Here refusal and the withdrawal of the self are fused with the phenomenon of drawing attention to the self and presenting the self in one indivisible act. By ornamenting ourselves or a part of ourselves, we conceal what is adorned. And by concealing it, we draw attention to it and its attractions. This could be called an optical necessity which incorporates the simultaneity of consent and refusal—the formula of all flirtation—into the first stage of the development of clothing as well.

If we go deeper into this matter, we might claim that the entire dualism of this attitude is only the phenomenon or the empirical technique for the realization of a mode of conduct that is basically completely unified. I shall examine the nature of this unity later. Here, I shall only draw the conclusion that this concomitance of consent and refusal cannot be a static juxtaposition but must be a vital exchange, an intertwined form of mutual reference. Where this does not succeed, semi-concealment does not attain its significance as flirtation either but rather exhibits a disagreeable contradiction.

The complex aesthetic-psychological problem of why so many modes of sensibility find something quite unbearable in the pose of the Medici Venus can be solved on this basis. Her effort to cover herself with her hand is an attempt that employs unsatisfactory means. In fact, she stands there quite naked, and the intended concealment is—we might say—unorganically related to this fact. The pose exhibits an intrinsically integral attitude with reference to exposure, an alternation between submission and denial, as flirtation requires. The cause of this—or perhaps its effect—is that this figure leaves the sphere of art and enters that of reality. It is not the aesthetic image of a woman who, attempting to cover herself, flirts with an ideal spectator who exists in the same unreal space. On the contrary, we feel as if she were flirting with the real spectator standing before her, as if a scene from life were being played out here—except that the woman happens to be made of marble rather than of flesh and bone.

Consider the fact that, for this *real* spectator, she is not veiled at all. Through symbolism, that would be possible for the ideal spectator. However, this holds true exclusively in the sphere of *art*, which is not valid for this case. In light of this consideration, gestures that are meant to veil her appear as an incoherent desire to submit and withdraw, a collapse of the polar moments of flirtation into two different spheres. As a result, the meaning of the pose is frustrated, so that we are offended rather than delighted.

One of the most typical cases of the practice of flirtation lies in the domain of *intellectual* self-concealment: the assertion of something that is not really meant, the paradox whose authenticity remains doubtful, the threat that is not seriously intended, the self-disparagement of fishing for compliments. Oscillation between affirmation and the denial of genuineness is always responsible for the charm exercised by this sort of conduct. The listener does not know whether the speaker is being truthful or is acting in a contrary fashion. As a result, the subject of this sort of flirtation leaves tangible reality and enters a vacillating and fluctuating category in which his real being can be included but not clearly grasped.

A scale of graduated phenomena leads from the assertion that is really made in complete seriousness, in which only a touch of self-irony is barely perceptible, to the paradox or the outrageous humility that leaves us in doubt as to whether the speaker is making a fool of himself or of us. However, each stage on this scale can be put to the use of flirtation, by men as well as women. This is because the subject stands behind his expression in a semi-veiled fashion and gives us the feeling that he seems to offer himself and to slip through our hands at almost the same moment.

Even so, it seems that flirtation as a consciously dualistic form of conduct stands in complete contradiction to that "uniformity" of the female nature which—regardless of how it is understood and how profoundly or superficially it is interpreted—runs through every psychology of women as its basic theme. Wherever we perceive an opposition between the nature of the male and female psyches as such, it tends to be the following: As regards her nature, woman is a being that is centralized in itself. Her impulses and ideas are most closely concentrated around a single point or a few points and can be more directly stimulated by these points than is the case for man, who is more differentiated and whose interests and activities take place in a more objectively defined autonomy, differentiated by the division of labor from the totality and the interior of the personality.

It will become clear that the centralized nature of woman does not run counter to the dualism of flirtation and that her relationship to the male in flirtation represents a distinctive synthesis of the crucial aspects of this relationship. This is because, as regards its specific and incomparable meaning, it is precisely the relationship of the woman to the man that is exhausted by the processes of concession and denial. There are, of course, innumerable other relationships between them: friendship and enmity, a commonality of interests and moral solidarity, a common bond under the aegis of religious or social considerations, and cooperation for either objective or personal reasons. However these are general human relationships that essentially can take place between members of the same sex as well; or they are determined by some real or ideal point that lies outside the subjects themselves and the direct lines of connection between them. In that case, they do not form a reciprocal interaction between the subjects as pure and exclusive as that which holds true for refusal and concession—which are obviously to be understood in their most comprehensive sense, including all contents, both internal and external.[1]

Refusing and conceding are things that women, and only women, can do in a consummate fashion. On the basis of this observation, there has been an attempt to derive the entire fact of flirtation from the ancient—and in its scope, of course, quite indeterminate—phenomenon of "marriage by abduction." Nevertheless, even today there are completely different peoples around the world—the Tun-

---

1. In investigations that concern the entire scope of the relationship between the sexes, it is practically unavoidable—for obvious psychological reasons—that expressions primarily take on their crudest possible sense. However, when we speak of concession and pleasure, consent and refusal, in this context, we refer to the general forms of that relationship, which have the most lofty moral and aesthetic components as well as the most base. Despite these extreme differences in values, from a purely psychological perspective these formal categories have the same force.

gus, the New Zealanders, and some Bedouin tribes—among whom it is regarded as eminently appropriate for the bride to resist the bridegroom with all her powers on the journey home and to submit only after a violent struggle. This has the elements of flirtation, of course, even if in brutal proportions. However, with a change in scale, it seems that the properties of flirtation also change: Although the bride resists, she also surrenders. The coquette, by comparison, neither resists, nor does she surrender.

In refusing and conceding, the attitudes of the sexes are quite characteristically different. When a man refuses a woman who makes advances to him, this may be thoroughly justified, or even necessary, on ethical, personal, or aesthetic grounds. However, there is always something awkward, unchivalrous, and in a certain sense blameworthy about it. For the woman in this case, a rebuff can easily assume a tragic character. It is not proper for a man to reject a woman, regardless of whether it was improper for her to offer herself to him. In the other direction, however, the balance is struck perfectly clearly: Rebuffing the zealous suitor is, so to say, a thoroughly appropriate gesture for the woman. And yet at the same time—and in spite of a reservation that will be indicated at the conclusion of this essay—the woman's capacity to surrender herself is such a profound, total, and exhaustive expression of her being that perhaps it can never be attained by a man in this way. In saying no and saying yes, in surrendering and refusing to surrender themselves, women are the masters.

This is the consummation of the sexual role that belongs to the female throughout the animal kingdom: to be the *chooser*. It is probably the basis of a phenomenon observed by Darwin: among our household pets, the females exhibit a much more individual attraction and aversion toward the males than the males demonstrate for the females. Since the woman is the chooser she is influenced much more by the individuality of the man than he is by hers. The fact that the man has this or that specific characteristic is responsible for her choice. The man, however, is more disposed to pursue the woman as woman—within the limits that civilization may also modify this fundamental relationship from both sides. This individual selection, which is the lot of the woman, gives her much more opportunity than the man has to leave the choice in abeyance. Thus it is no wonder that out of all these moments of flirtation, a form develops for women that does not suit men at all. In this form, there is a sense in which refusal and concession are simultaneously possible for women.

Reduced to its *most general* formulation, the motive responsible for this conduct on the part of the woman is the fascination of freedom and power. Normally there are only one or two occasions on which the woman is in a position to decide the fundamental questions of her life. And even in these crucial cases, the individual freedom of her resolution is quite often only apparent. In flirtation, however, there is a sense in which she chronically takes on this decision, even if only in a symbolic and approximate fashion. Suppose she creates the impression that consent and refusal, inclination and aversion either dominate one another by turns or have the same force. In that case, she withdraws herself from both and manipulates each as an instrument, behind which her own unbiased personality stands in complete freedom.

It is a universally confirmed observation that freedom does not remain limited to its negative sense but, rather, immediately or simultaneously tends to be used for the acquisition and exercise of power. In the case of flirtation, these two senses become directly and inextricably interrelated. The power of the woman in relation to the man is exhibited in consent *or* refusal. It is precisely this antithesis—in which the conduct of the flirt alternates—that grounds the feeling of freedom, the independence of the self from the one as well as the other, the autonomous existence that lies beyond the dominated oppositions. The power of the woman over consent and refusal is *prior* to the decision. Once she has decided, in either direction, her power is ended. Flirtation is a means of enjoying this power in an enduring form. And at least in a number of cases, it can be observed that women who are very domineering are also very flirtatious.

To clarify the typology of the situation, it should be stressed that all this hesitation and vacillation does not affect the being of the woman and the determinate quality of its alignment at all but only its discernability for her partner. There is no sense in which this betrays an objective and inner uncertainty on the part of the woman. Where this is the case, it produces a picture quite different from flirtation. Either this picture is only superficially similar to flirtation or, in a certain embarrassment, it takes refuge in the forms of flirtation, perhaps in order to gain time for the decision. Inwardly, the flirtatious woman is completely resolved in either one direction or the other. The meaning of the entire situation lies only in the fact that she has to conceal her resolve and that, as regards something that is intrinsically certain, she can place her partner in a state of uncertainty or vacillation which holds true only for *him*. It is this that gives the flirt her power and her superiority: the fact that *she* is resolved and determined within herself, as a result of which an understanding obtains between her and the man that uproots *him* and makes *him* uncertain.

Consider the fact that the man whose desire is captivated by the favor of the woman gives himself over to this game, and not merely because he has no other alternative. On the contrary, it is frequently as if he found a peculiar enticement and delight precisely in the fickle manner in which he is treated. In the first place, this is quite obviously a consequence of the well-known phenomenon that a sequence of experience oriented to a final feeling of happiness radiates a part of its eudaemonistic value onto the moments of the sequence that precede this final moment. Flirtation is one of the most trenchant cases of this experience. Originally, the only pleasure in the erotic sequence may have been physiological. The pleasure, however, has gradually come to include all the earlier moments of the sequence as well. Insofar as a purely psychological issue is at stake here, it is probable that a historical evolution has in fact taken place. This is because the meaning of pleasure extends to moments of the erotic domain which are all the more remote, allusive, and symbolic as the personality is more refined and cultivated. This process of psychic retreat can go so far that, for example, a young man in love draws more bliss from the first secret clasp of the hand than from any subsequent unconditional concession; and for many delicate and sensitive natures—who are by no means necessarily frigid or chaste—the kiss, or even the mere consciousness of the return of love, surpasses what might be called the more substantial erotic delights. In her interest in him and her desire to attract him, the man with whom a woman flirts already feels the somehow allusive charm of possessing her, in quite the same way that the promise of happiness already anticipates a part of the happiness attained.

There is a further nuance of this relationship that acts with an independent force. Wherever the value of a final goal is already perceptible in its means or its preliminary stages, the quantum of the value that is enjoyed is modified by the following fact: There is no real sequence in which what is gained in an intermediate stage guarantees with absolute certainty that the decisive terminal value will also be obtained. The bill for this, which we have discounted with the foretaste of pleasure, may never be honored. In addition to an unavoidable reduction in the value of the intermediate stages, this also results in an increase in their value as a result of the fascination of risk, especially if the element of fate—which is inaccessible to a decision that lies within our own power and is intrinsic to all that we attain—heightens its mysterious attraction. If we calculated on the basis of its completely objective weight the chance of failure that lies between a preliminary stage and the final stage, then it would hardly come to an antedating of good fortune. But we also experience chance as an allure, an enticing gamble for the favor of the incalculable powers.

In the psychic conduct that the flirt understands how to provoke, there is a sense in which this eudaemonistic value of risk—the knowledge that one does not know whether he will succeed or fail—has been arrested and stabilized. On the one hand, this conduct draws anticipated happiness from the promise that flirtation implies. The reverse of this, on the other hand, the chance that anticipation may be disappointed by a change in the situation, results from the remoteness that the flirt makes her partner feel at the same time. Insofar as both are continually played off against each other, so that neither is sufficiently serious to repress the other from consciousness, the possibility of the Perhaps still stands above the Negative. Indeed, this Perhaps, in which the passivity of submitting and the activity of succeeding form a unity of enticement, circumscribes the entire inner response to the behavior of the flirt.

Suppose that by virtue of his delight in risk and the characteristic concrete intermeshing of its polar possibilities, the reaction of the man signifies much more than simply being carried along with the oscillation of the game of flirtation. In that case, when he begins to play the game itself and is attracted by it, not by one of its possible definitive results, then ultimately his role far surpasses the status of a mere object. The entire action is really elevated into the sphere of play only under this condition. As long as the man still takes it seriously, it intersects with the sphere of reality. Now the man will go no further than the limits specified by flirtation. In view of the logical and genetic meaning of flirtation, this seems to nullify its concept. Actually, however, it produces the case that exhibits the pure form of flirtation, detached from every deviation and all prospect of change. It is less the art of *pleasing*—which is still somehow projected into the sphere of reality—than the *art* of pleasing that constitutes the pivotal point of the relationship and its attractions. Here flirtation completely relinquishes the role of an instrument or a mere provisional entity and assumes that of an ultimate value.

All the hedonistic value that flirtation acquired from the first role is extended into this second role. The provisional quality of flirtation has lost its quality of being conditioned by something final, or even by the idea of something final. Consider the fact that flirtation has this cachet of the provisional, of suspension and indecision. Although a logical contradiction, this is a psychological fact. It is the ultimate attraction of flirtation, in which there is no inquiry beyond the moment of its existence. This is why the consequence of flirtatious behavior—an uncertainty and uprootedness on the part of the man, a surrender to a Perhaps that is often full of despair, corresponding to the inner certainty of the flirt—is completely transformed into its opposite in this case. Where the man himself wants nothing more than this stage, it is precisely the conviction that the flirt is not serious that gives him a certain assurance in relation to her. Where consent is not desired and refusal is not feared—and yet also where the possible obstacles to his longing do not need to be considered—he can abandon himself to the fascination of this game more completely than would be the case if he wished—or perhaps somehow feared as well—that the path once taken also led to the final point.

This is no more than the clearest expression of the relationship between art and play, which is invariably characteristic of flirtation. Kant's claim about the nature of art—that it is "purposiveness without purpose"—holds true for flirtation to the greatest extent possible. The work of art has no "purpose" at all. However, its parts seem to be so significant and inextricably interrelated, with each necessarily in its place, that it is as if they worked together to realize a completely specifiable purpose. The flirt acts exactly as if she were interested only in the man who happens to be her partner, as if her conduct should culminate in complete surrender, regardless of how qualified this surrender may be. However, this logical, purposive sense of her conduct—as it might be called—is not her own view at all. On the contrary, she leaves her conduct suspended in space in an inconsistent fashion by giving it an aim that is oriented in a completely different direction: to please, to captivate, to be desired, but without allowing herself to be taken seriously in any way. She proceeds in a thoroughly purposive fashion but repudiates the "purpose" to which her conduct would have to lead in the sequence of reality, sublimating it into the purely subjective delights of play.

Of course what differentiates the inner or what might be called transcendental nature of flirtation from that of art is the following consideration. From the outset, art places itself beyond reality. It frees itself from reality by means of a perspective that is utterly averse to reality. While it is true that flirtation also does no more than *play* with reality, yet it is still *reality* with which it plays. The oscillation of impulse that it offers and calls forth never draws its fascination entirely from the purely detached forms of consent and refusal, from what could be called the abstract relationship of the sexes—even though this would be the real, albeit never completely attainable, consummation of flirtation. There is always a reminder of sensibilities whose home is to be found only in the sequence of reality. The pure relation of forms is suffused with them. It is true that the flirt and—in the case indicated in the foregoing—her partner as well play with, and in this respect detach themselves from, reality. Unlike the artist, however, they do not play with the appearance of reality but rather with reality itself.

In one respect, of course, a characteristic analogy between flirtatious behavior and art still obtains. It is said that art is "indifferent to its object." The meaning of this assertion can only be that the values art extracts from things are not altered in any fashion by the fact that these same things, measured on the basis of non-aesthetic standards, are delightful or distasteful, moral or immoral, religious or profane. There is a sense in which flirtation assumes this relatively simple manner of situating itself beyond the other positive or negative values of the phenomenal sphere. As we indicated above in a different context, the activity of the flirt in relation to the things that are instruments of her intentions is an ideal oscillation—that is, it is at least perceived as a constant possibility—between interest and indifference toward these instruments, submission to an object alternating with its opposite, and attraction to and repulsion of every single thing.

Consider this detachment from the objective value significance of things and their value significance in other respects as it is expressed in simultaneous positive and negative behavior toward them. Once again, it is clearly defined in the impartiality with which the flirt places all objective polarities of every sort at her disposal: an inviting as well as a discouraging glance, piety as well as atheism, naiveté as well as sophistication, knowledge as well as ignorance—indeed, a woman can flirt with her flirtatious conduct itself just as well as she can flirt with her non-flirtatious conduct. In the same way that all things must be at the disposal of the artist because he wants nothing from them except their form, so they must also be at the disposal of the flirt because she wants only to incorporate them into the game of holding and releasing, compliance and aversion.

Again, a woman may attempt to ensnare a man by means of her religiosity or by means of her iconoclasm. This is not yet flirtation. It becomes flirtation only by virtue of that distinctive mode of conduct that does not submit to any content as final. Flirtation does not abdicate its sovereign right to say yes or no to this content to anyone else, and it allows its characteristic means of attracting its partner— the coincidence of enticement and rejection—to color its relationship to things as well. Here too, the Perhaps—watching something and ignoring it at the same time, the freedom in relation to means that are of no intrinsic significance and thus are not taken seriously— stands as a backdrop against the attitude of seriousness, no matter how pronounced it may be at the moment.

Art achieves transcendence of the real significance of things by inquiring exclusively into their form with an unequivocal confidence. This is why art is always determinate, and a flirtation with art is always an embarrassment and a blunder. For flirtation, on the other hand, this same transcendence develops in the following way: While it does indeed periodically take up that real significance, it is nullified at every moment by means of its antithesis, even if only as a possibility, an allusion, a nuance, a background. From the standpoint of the other categories and objective contents of life, art can appear as play because it is ruthlessly serious about one category that excludes all these others. Flirtation, on the other hand, is play because it does not take anything seriously. However, this negative way of expressing the matter is a thoroughly positive way of proceeding. At least potentially, it plays off all oppositions against one another and in a certain sense relieves the relationship in which they are situated from every burden of a decision.

Compared with the Platonic categories with which this essay began, art stands equally above both having and not-having. It has all things insofar as it wants only their form and their artistic meaning. And it has nothing since reality, the object of genuine "having," holds no interest at all for it. As the Franciscans said of themselves, the arts are *omnia habentes, nihil possidentes*. Limited to the circumference of its object, flirtation is no less distant from having and not-having—or, actively expressed, from giving and not-giving. However, it does not stand above them but rather, one might say, between them, insofar as it maintains the interests that it has in both or gives to both in an unstable equilibrium; or it compounds them in such a way that one is always neutralized by the other, as in an infinite process.

Earlier I mentioned that the essential dualism of flirtation does not contradict that unity and resoluteness with which the woman as a type confronts the erotic question as an issue of All or Nothing. Here again, "All" is not limited to its surface meaning. There is no sense in which this contradiction obtains. This can be seen from the fact that, ultimately and finally, flirtation becomes the symbol for the mode in which that unity is exhibited. In other words, it seems to be the universal experience of the male sensibility that the woman— indeed, the deepest, most devoted woman, whose charm is inexhaustible—holds back some ultimate, indecipherable and unattainable quality even in the most passionate offering and disclosure of herself. Perhaps this is connected with that unity, in which all beginnings and possibilities reside beside or in one another in intimate and undifferentiated fashion. As a result, we feel in relation to most women a certain lack of development, of adequate actualization of potencies. Moreover, this feeling obtains quite independently of whatever obstacles to development may be presented by social prejudices and impediments.

It is, of course, a mistake to regard this "lack of differentiation" simply as a deficiency and a condition of inferiority. On the contrary, it is the thoroughly positive mode of being of the woman, which forms its own ideal and has no less legitimacy than the "differentiated state" of the man. From the perspective of the man, however, the woman's mode of being appears as a Not-Yet, an unredeemed promise, an unborn profusion of obscure possibilities that have not yet developed far enough beyond their psychic location to become visible and apprehensible.

A further point also has the same consequence. The modes of formation and expression—by no means merely linguistic—that our culture places at the disposal of the psychic interior have essentially been created by men. For this reason, it is inevitable that they are primarily of use to the male mode of being and its needs. Thus, even for the differentially female, there are countless occasions on which there will simply be no satisfactory and intelligible expression. This also contributes to the feeling that even the most complete surrender of the woman does not eliminate a final secret reservation of her soul, the feeling that something whose disclosure and presentation would really be expected will not detach itself from its ultimate basis. This is not, of course, an intentional limitation on liberality, something that the beloved would be begrudged, but rather an ultimate quality of the personality that simply cannot be explicated. It too is surrendered, but not as something transparent that can be identified. It is a locked receptacle for which the recipient has no key. Thus it is not surprising if the feeling arises in the recipient that something is being withheld from him, if the feeling of not possessing something is interpreted as if it had not been given.

Regardless of how this phenomenon of reserve originally developed, it represents a mysterious interpenetration of consent and refusal, of giving and rejecting, that in a certain sense prefigures flirtation. Suppose that flirtation incorporates this "semi-concealment" of the woman, which expresses her most profound relationship to the man, with a conscious emphasis. This alone explains why there is no sense in which flirtation is a "strategem of the prostitute," so little that there is no sense in which either the courtesan or the most unspiritual and sensual woman tends to be the most flirtatious. It also explains the fact that men for whom every purely surface enticement remains utterly without effect surrender to the charm of flirtation consciously and with emotion. And it explains the fact that flirtation debases neither its subject nor its object.

A more profound sense of the interpretation of love as an intermediate state between having and not-having is disclosed in this form, which molds the interest of the woman in the relationship between the sexes—in this consent and refusal, which is the basis of all consent and refusal. Now not-having grows into having. Both form aspects of a relational unity, the most extreme and passionate form of which ultimately lies in having something that one at the same time does not have. In the relationship between the sexes, the profound metaphysical loneliness of the individual—for the surmounting of which all the fondness of one person for another is only a path that leads to infinity—has achieved a distinctively colored configuration, but perhaps most fundamentally, a tangible configuration. Here as elsewhere, the relationship between the sexes provides the prototype for countless relationships between the individual and the interindividual life. It appears as the purest example of so many processes because, from the outset, the form of these processes is defined by that fundamental limiting condition of our life.

Consider, for example, the fact that our intellect can never comprehend all becoming and evolution, real as well as logical, on the basis of a complete unity. On the contrary, in itself such a unity remains sterile and without an intelligible ground for the phenomenon of becoming different. This is probably related to the fact that the origin of our life is conditioned by the concomitant functioning of two principles. Even the fact that the human is a dualistic being—with his life and thought moving in the form of a polarity, every existential content determined by and finding itself only in its antithesis—is perhaps a consequence of that ultimate fissure of the human species, the elements of which eternally seek one another, complement one another, and yet never overcome their own opposition. Consider the fact that the human being, with his most passionate needs, is dependent upon that being from whom he is perhaps separated by the deepest metaphysical chasm. This is the purest image—but perhaps also the crucially decisive original form—for the loneliness of the human being, who is ultimately an alien, not only in relation to the things of the world, but also in relation to those to whom he is closest.

If this is why concomitant having and not-having is the impenetrable external form, and often the ultimate basis, of the erotic, then the erotic is distilled from this form by means of flirtation. There is a sense in which this happens in the form of play, just as play as its contents frequently constitutes the simplest fundamental relationships from the complexities of reality; pursuing and winning, danger and the chance of happiness, struggle and deception. By means of the conscious quality of flirtation, each of these opposing elements— which penetrate deeply into one another—is exhibited more clearly in its antithesis. There is a sense in which flirtation lends a positive concreteness to not-having, making it tangible for the first time by means of the playful, suggestive illusion of having, just as, conversely, flirtation intensifies the attraction of having to the most extreme degree by means of the threatening illusion of not-having. And if this fundamental relationship shows that in definitive having, there is still a sense in which we do not have, flirtation ensures that in definitive not-having, there is still a sense in which we can have. A French social psychologist offers an explanation of flirtation that concludes with a similar idea. With the advance of culture, increased sensitivity, on the one hand, and the equally large increase in the number of provocative phenomena, on the other, have produced an erotic repression in men. It is simply not possible to possess all the attractive women—whereas in primitive times, such as abundance of attractive phenomena just did not exist. Flirtation is a remedy for this condition. By this means, the woman could give herself— potentially, symbolically, or by approximation—to a large number of men, and in this same sense, the individual man could possess a large number of women.

If it seemed that flirtation developed exclusively in the relationship between men and women—a surface reflection which, refracted from a certain angle, represents the ultimate ground of this relationship—then in the final analysis the ubiquitous experience that a large number of generally human forms of conduct would have their normative paradigm in the relation of the sexes proves this. If we consider the modes in which the person encounters things and

other persons, then among these, flirtation qualifies as a thoroughly
general, formal mode of conduct that does not exclude any content.
There are countless occasions on which the consent or refusal with
which we confront decisions of an important or a routine sort—
submission and self-interest, taking sides on an issue, or faith in a
person or a doctrine—is transformed into a consent and a refusal, or
into an alternation between the two which has the character of
simultaneous coexistence because the alternative stands as a possibility or a temptation behind any given decision.

Linguistic usage allows us to "flirt" with religious or political
positions, with important matters as well as with amusements. Moreover, the conduct thus designated takes place in beginnings and
mere nuances, in admixtures with other kinds of conduct, and with
self-deception concerning its character much more frequently than
language will allow. Consider the charms of the simultaneous For
and Against, the Perhaps, the protracted reservation of the decision
which permits a foretaste of the enjoyment of both its aspects
together, aspects which in their realization are mutually exclusive.
All this is not only characteristic of the flirtation of a woman with a
man. On the contrary, it plays upon thousands of other contents. This
is the form in which the indecisiveness of life is crystallized into a
thoroughly positive way of acting. Although it does not make a
virtue of this necessity, it does make it into a pleasure. The soul has
found the appropriate form for its relationship to countless things in
that playful approach and withdrawal—even though it is certainly
not always accompanied by the attitude of "play"—in the act of
taking hold of something only in order to let it fall again, of letting it
fall only to take hold of it again, in what could be called the tentative
turning toward something on which the shadow of its own denial
already falls.

Although the moralist may censure this, it is a part of the problematic of life that there are many things with regard to which life has no
unambiguous, a priori, settled locus, even though life cannot simply
repudiate a relationship to them. Because of its own characteristic
form, life does not fit properly into the place that these things
provide for our conduct and sensibilities. This is the source of the
approach and withdrawal, the tentative retention and release in
whose precarious dualism that fundamental relationship of having

and not-having—which is often quite unavoidable—is painted. Because such a tragic moment of life can clothe itself in the playful, precarious form, lacking all commitments, that we call flirting with things, we understand that this form achieves its most typical and purest fulfillment precisely in the relationship between the sexes—in the relationship that conceals within itself perhaps the most mysterious and tragic relation of life in its ultimate ecstasy and most glittering attraction.

ON LOVE (A FRAGMENT)

Between the I and the Thou, the first conflict arises for the human consciousness, and the first consolidation as well. The temporal priority of this relationship has the consequence that it subsequently qualifies as what might be called the absolute material on which, in the final analysis, our decisions and valuations, the justice and injustice of our praxis, and the claims upon us are made good. Ultimately, every intention of our conduct is exhausted in the alternation between egoism and altruism, which assume countless modifications and means, guises and consequences. Even when it is subordinated to objective ideals—as in Plato, Thomas Aquinas, Kant, and socialism—egoism is still more or less clearly designated as the immanent counterprinciple. The immediate concrete demand, however, even if not the abstract demand, always has a Thou, personal or trans-individual, as its content. It is the general opinion that the choice between egoism and altruism is made on the level of eudaemonism as the source of its content. Aside from the fact that there is no sense in which this level comprises all the dimensions in which these concepts can be extended, even the most complete extension ascribed to them is incapable of adequately expressing our real ultimate motivations.

At this point, I shall only take note of an argument that lies off the path of our present inquiry. There are countless occasions on which our will is concerned with objective formations of existence in such a way that a state, an event, or an aspect of things is simply supposed to exist, without giving any consideration at all to the result that the realization of this intention has for an I or a Thou. This thoroughly objective intention, which lies beyond every I and Thou and their unreconciled or reconciled dualism, seems to me to be an undeniable and quite distinctively human fact. And in the sense that this fact lies above that dualism, another fact lies beneath it: purely impulsive behavior. If we call it egoistic when someone follows his impulses in an unconstrained fashion, then we elevate his behavior above its own sphere into another, in which an altruistic claim is raised. Because his behavior does not, of course, satisfy this demand, it appears as egoistic. In itself, however, it has this property no more than the growth of a plant or the falling of a stone, both of which follow their own purely distinctive laws, can be called egoistic. Quite rightly, egoism always signifies a teleological orientation—to some sort of reaction of the Ego. In calling an action egoistic, we implicitly presuppose such an orientation, which, however, it is precisely the nature of the impulse to resist. And yet its content can be directly linked with the well-being of a Thou, the destruction of the I, or with something that is teleologically completely senseless; for the claim that impulses signify adaptations that are of use only to the subject does not even hold true physiologically, much less psychologically.

Suppose that on the basis of these simple cases we have grasped the possible independence of our conduct from the alternative of egoism and altruism. In that event we shall also be able to penetrate that more complicated relationship—whose reductive power, however, is no less severe—in which conduct is motivated "out of love." If we call an action altruistic in the strict sense when it is for the benefit of a person whom we find quite indifferent or unsympathetic, even hostile, then action out of love cannot properly be characterized in the same way. Our own impulse is too narrow and our own satisfaction too closely interwoven with it to simply transpose its *Telos* onto the Thou. For the same reason, the concept of egoism will not work here either. Aside from all the selflessness that lies in the material content of action out of love, the concept of egoism would not conform to its nobility and value. Finally, from the perspective of its ultimate source, action out of love is too integral and continuous to qualify as some sort of mechanical composite of both motivations.

Thus the only remaining possibility is to regard motivation on the basis of love as distinctive and primary, unaffected by that usual reduction. The fact that the question concerning this reduction is inappropriate in this context follows from the consideration that a rationalistic psychology can either enthrone action out of love as altruistic or degrade it as fundamentally egoistic with apparently the same justification. It is also relevant that in this context the relationship between purpose and impulse is quite distinctive. Suppose that

I accede to the wishes of another person because I regard them as worthy and just. In that case, action in accordance with the justice of these wishes is my ultimate purpose, and the realization of this justice is my own decisive motive. Suppose I do the same thing because I love the person. As regards the phenomenon in question, the condition of this person which is to be brought about is still my ultimate purpose. And yet it is not my real motive. On the contrary, my real motive is my love, the motive force of which is only transformed into this *Telos*—however, as this might be expressed, by itself alone. In all other cases our action, regardless of whether its basis invariably has a positive value, is separated from its ultimate motive by a certain distance. This does not hold true for love, for which the following differentiating factor is decisive: Love for another person as what might be called the general motive for a particular action is more indivisibly connected with its content and permeates it much more directly than holds true for any other motivation with the possible exception of hate.

There is a sense in which we come from a greater distance when we do someone a good turn because of morality or inner acquiescence, religion, or social solidarity than when we do this because of love. The character of the good deed, with its tension between the I and the Thou, simply does not appear in the same clearcut fashion here. That is because the I has felt its way across the hiatus to the Thou. The existential will of the I flows to the Thou with complete intimacy. It does not need a bridge, which separates just as it connects.

Nevertheless, the dynamic at stake here is different from the metaphysical unity of all being as such, from which Schopenhauer, for example, derives charity and sacrifice. This is precisely the miracle of love. It does not nullify the being-for-itself of either the I or the Thou. On the contrary, it makes this being-for-itself into a condition under which that nullification of distance and the egoistic reversion of the existential will to itself follow. This is a completely irrational phenomenon that resists the categories of logic, which in other respects hold valid. Schopenhauer's proposed explanation of this nullification of distance by means of the transcendent unity of being is a form of rationalism. His failure to comprehend the nature of love, which will be discussed below, is above all exhibited here.

On the basis of the retrospective consideration of those categories, action out of love can, of course, be ascribed to the correlation of egoism and altruism just as well as to that of impulse and teleology. However, this would misrepresent its real inner nature, just as when the longing of the lover for physical union with the beloved is degraded to a mere "sexual drive."

From the perspective which implicates the genuinely impulsive more intimately within the teleological, love in its specifically erotic sense and the conduct that conforms to it have been explained as a confluence of the two fountainheads of sensuality and sentiment. However, the crucial unity is also missing from this dualism of elements. It obviously remains nothing more than a mere manner of speaking if we can say only that sensuality and sentiment form a unity in love. That is because it would be necessary to identify the force that interrelates or links these two quite heterogeneous psychic elements. In that case, the essence of love would lie in this force, which differs from both elements and could not be mechanically constructed as a composite from a part of one and a part of the other—just as their mechanistic character is precisely the fundamental error of all such attempts to constitute an integral entity that has its origin in life on the basis of pre-existing elements.

For this reason, it would be much better to assume that the activity of sensuality and the activity of sentiment constitute two of the consequences of this unity; they arise either on the surface of consciousness or in their union with the manifold of the natural and the given. There is a sense in which they are prismatic reductions that our inner organization undertakes to perform on the homogeneous erotic fact. There are countless occasions on which our intellect is unable to comprehend a unified entity. As a result, we are obliged to break it down into several elements on the basis of a guess, a stipulation, or an intuition, and reconstitute it as a "synthetic unity" only by means of an amalgam of these elements. In the same way, our emotional reality also seems to be an integral and immanently continuous entity. However, as soon as it appears on the surface of our life—which in every sense is practical and multidimensional—it disintegrates into a multiplicity of individual feelings. But if we focus on its unity, we see it in a combination, a self-supplementation, and an interweaving of these differentiated elements.

It is not intellectual reduction which is at stake here (although this can be the case *as well*) but rather an emotional development that is experienced. The multiplicity of feelings that arise from faith in God, the often divergent sensations with which we react to a work of art, the distinctive "mix" of feelings that an encounter with an individual often produces in us, the emotional conflation and confusion of inner impulses that appear when we engage in a total evaluation of our own self—I am inclined to regard all these cases as secondary phenomena, the analytical precipitates of a way of acting and a subjective orientation that are in themselves completely homogeneous.

Finally, consider the inner reality which, in this emotional phenomenon, is always a *single* entity: *one* fate, *one* result, *one* act. The question of whether we propose to call this reality itself a feeling or regard it as an indefinable and subconscious mode of acting and being is a purely verbal issue. It seems to me that the first of these views is correct. As regards the cleavage whose products are given to us as feelings, I see no reason that we should presuppose a fundamental process for it that is generally different from these feelings. A phenomenon of this sort seems to obtain when the erotic relationship is understood as the synthesis of something that is intrinsically sensual and something that is intrinsically emotional. In that case, the combination of both on the conscious level of experience represents the unity from which they emanated. It is the inner mode of being— in itself, completely indivisible—that we call love.

I shall not pursue these relationships any further in this context, which is concerned only with refuting the possibility of constructing love—as this might be expressed—from a plurality of factors none of which is love itself. Once love exists, elements of the most diverse description may become linked with it. As a result, a total phenomenon composed of many members may appear under its name. However, love itself is a psychic act that cannot be analyzed in this way, nor can it be understood as a consequence of any combination of other elements. The diversity of the many phenomena that language designates by means of the concept of love does not speak against their fundamental unity. On the contrary, it shows that such a unity must obtain. Consider a fact for whose mere occurrence one element requires the appearance of another. It is extremely improbable that such a fact would form the unchanging nucleus of such an immense profusion of constantly changing processes. The love of God and love for the fatherland; Christian charity and the love between man and wife; the love for a friend and the rational-practical love of the humanitarian ideal—they are already sufficiently diverse. In addition, however, we also legitimately speak of the love for inanimate things, not only for ideals and styles of life, but for landscapes, utilitarian objects, and works of art as well. If I "love" the landscape of Florence, this does not mean that I would like to live there permanently. Nor does it mean that I am aesthetically impressed by it. Both may be the case. However, neither what could be called the practical subjective enjoyment of this landscape nor an objective value judgment of it—taken alone or acting concomitantly—can qualify as the distinctive inner attitude that I designate with the expression of love for this landscape.

It seems that even the mystery of sexual eroticism lies in the fact that we actually *love* the *body* of the other person in this sense; we do not merely "want" it and contemplate it only aesthetically. Desire and esteem may be *connected* with love. In comparison with its posture vis-à-vis the object, however, not only desire but—considered exactly—also esteem come "too close" to the object. The one is a matter of the exercise of power over the object, the other a matter of an authoritative decision concerning the object. Love remains aloof from both possibilities.

The love for an inanimate object may exhibit with distinctive clarity the relationship of the subject to an object that we call love, a relationship that is not comparable with anything else and which for this reason cannot be constructed from anything else. Here we see love in complete independence from all practical and theoretical considerations, and from all judgments of real value as well (for nothing prevents us from "loving" something that, objectively, is thoroughly indifferent, or even inferior). Here we see how love arises from the completely irrational depths of life, without, however, necessarily tending to advance or compromise this life in any way. Here we see love as a pure quality or dynamic of the subject. Nevertheless it is a category in which the real content of the object is grasped. As a result of this transcendental incomparability, the object of love lies in a formal subordinate order together with the object of knowledge, the object of faith, and the object of valuation. In loving the object, we consummate one configuration of the fundamental relationship between the soul and the world. It is true that the soul remains bound to its center. This is the source of its limits as well as of its dimensions. And yet this immanence is also the form in which the soul becomes transcendent and by virtue of which it can comprehend the contents of the world and incorporate them into itself. If the soul did not exist in itself, then it could not move beyond itself. This inescapably temporal expression does not signify an apparent process of succession but rather the fundamentally homogeneous nature of life.

Considered from the perspective of the subject-object concept, love is the most powerful manifestation of the psychic immanence of the conception of the world. In the process of knowledge as well as that of valuation, we feel ourselves irresistibly grasped by something that we call a norm, a standard, or a value—descriptions that remain quite incomplete and derivative—something that simply lies beyond subject and object. When we love, however, and especially when the object of our love, unlike everything with a human soul, does not bear within itself a latent intention that disposes it to become an object of love, we feel a definite freedom in the choice, mode, and extent of our subjective activity. And yet here too it is the *object* that we form with this activity. The movement of feeling has the form of an ellipse. The object is situated in one of its focal points, even though this ellipse as a whole remains enclosed within the immanence of feeling. Thus consider the maximally extreme point at which the intrinsic significance of the object approximates the limiting value of zero—indeed, it has actually reached this value. Even in this case, we may have a sense of that all-embracing indefinable entity that lies beyond the polar antithesis of the psyche and the world and yet even in the limiting case of love, still constitutes love, as a relationship of the psyche to the world.

Certain realities of the psyche as well as certain theoretical modes of thought are equally responsible for obscuring the fact that love is one of the great formative categories of existence. It is, of course, unquestionable that there are countless occasions on which the emotion of love displaces and misrepresents the objectively admissible picture of its object. In this sense, therefore, its "formative" quality is generally recognized. However, it is obviously acknowledged in such a way that love cannot occupy a comparable status alongside the other formative powers of the spirit. What really takes place in this case? Theoretical factors have produced—or so it is supposed— a "true" picture of the beloved. To this picture, the erotic factor is appended, retrospectively as it were, accentuating certain factors, eliminating others, and giving the whole a new coloration. In this case, therefore, it is only the precise qualitative definition of an existing picture that is altered, without leaving its theoretical plane and producing a categorically new entity.

This modification which love that already exists brings about in the objectively true idea has nothing to do with the primary creation that brings forth the beloved person as such. The person I perceive and know, the person I fear and admire, and the person the work of art has formed always constitute a distinctive entity. If we recognize the person who is an object of intellectual knowledge only as the person he is "in reality" and treat all those other modes as nothing more than diverse contexts in which we inwardly place this altered reality, this is due merely to the preeminent significance that the intellectual picture itself has for our practical conduct. As regards their meaning, all of these categories, regardless of when or under what circumstances they come into play, in fact have the same status. Love also belongs to these categories insofar as it constitutes its object as a completely genuine entity.

Externally and from the standpoint of the temporal order, it is obvious that the person must first exist and be an object of knowledge before he becomes an object of love. However, nothing is thereby undertaken with regard to the person who already exists. As such, he also remains unchanged. It is rather in the subject that a completely new fundamental category has acquired creative force. For the same reason that the other person is "my idea," he is also "my love." He is not an invariable element that enters the status of being loved just as it enters all other configurations, or to which love is, as this might be expressed, appended. On the contrary, as "my love," the other person is a primordial and integral entity that did not exist before.

Consider only the religious case. The god who is loved is precisely for this reason a different god than would be the case were he not loved, even if all the other attributes intrinsically ascribed to him remained the same. Even if he is loved because of certain qualities or potencies, these "grounds" of love still lie in a stratum that is quite different from the love itself. In comparison with the category they assume in the absence of our love, these "grounds" of love, together with the totality of god's nature, are perceived as falling under a completely new category as soon as love really comes into play. This holds true even if these "grounds" of love are "believed" in the same way in both categories. However, we have no need at all for precisely this foundation. Eckhart explicitly proclaims that we should not love God because of this or that specific quality or reason, but rather exclusively because He exists.

This claim unequivocally reveals love as an ungrounded and primary category. This is exactly the status love has insofar as it determines the total and ultimate essence of its object and creates it as this object, which prior to this did not exist. As one who loves, I *am* a different person than I was before, for it is not one or the other of my "aspects" or energies that loves but rather the entire person— which need not imply a perceptible change in any other *external manifestations*. In the same way, the beloved as such is also a different being, arising from a different a priori than the person as an object of knowledge or fear, indifference or esteem. There is an absolute connection, and not a mere association, between love and its object only in this way: The object of love in its complete categorical significance does not exist prior to the love itself but only by means of it. Only on this basis does it becomes quite clear that love—and, by extension, the entire bearing of the lover as such—is thoroughly integral and not compounded from different and otherwise existing elements.

Thus the attempts to regard love as a secondary entity—in the sense that it is motivated as a resultant of other primary psychic factors—appear quite mistaken. The level of human development to which love belongs is too advanced for us to be able to situate it in the same temporal and genetic stratum as eating, breathing, or the sexual drive. Nor can we escape by means of the following obvious expedient: Although it is true that, from the perspective of its metaphysical import and its timeless significance, love belongs to the primary or ultimate order of values and ideas, its human or psychological realization exhibits a late stage of a long, continuous, and many-faceted developmental sequence of life. We cannot be satisfied with this mutually alien character of the meanings or responses of love. The problem of the dualism of love is acknowledged and clearly formulated in this way, but not solved. To conclude the problem at this point would be to despair of its solution.

In what follows, I shall return to the most general concept of love. This goes beyond the sexual phenomenon of love to include not only what transpires between one person and another but also what holds valid for all possible contents of the world. It seems to me of the utmost importance to recognize that loving is an immanent—or, as I am inclined to put it—a formal function of psychic life. Of course love is also actualized in an impulse that has its source in the world. However, love makes no a priori determination concerning the bearers of this impulse. This feeling is more completely bound up with the comprehensive unity of life than many others, perhaps than most others. The majority of our feelings of pleasure and pain, respect and contempt, fear and interested concern arise and have their life at a remote distance from the point at which the currents of subjective life flow together; or, more correctly, from the point at which, as their center, they rise. Even when we "love" an inanimate object—instead of characterizing it as useful, pleasing, or charming—we imply that there is a focal sensation that it awakens in us, even though the force of this feeling may vary considerably. These other valuations, on the other hand, correspond to more peripheral reactions. In the final analysis, I think that the existence of interested concerns, sensations, and inner implications beside a feeling of love is not correctly expressed as a differentiation of provinces of the psyche. On the contrary, I believe that under all conditions, love is a function of the relatively undifferentiated totality of life. These other cases only exhibit a more modest degree of its intensity.

It could be said that love is always a dynamic produced by an inner self-sufficiency. Although it is indeed transposed from a latent state into an actual state by means of its external object, it cannot be evoked in the strict sense. Either the psyche possesses love as an ultimate fact or it does not possess it at all. We cannot go behind love to any sort of external or internal motivating factor that would be more than what could be called its occasional cause. This is the most profound reason why it is utterly senseless to demand some sort of legitimate basis for love. I am not even certain whether its actualization always depends upon an object, or whether what is called the yearning or the need for love, the vague and diffuse urge, especially among young people, for something that could be loved, does not already qualify as love, a love that moves only within itself, in a sense love idling.

It is probably possible to regard the impulse for behavior as the emotional side of the beginning of the behavior itself. The fact that we feel ourselves "impelled" to perform an action means that inwardly the action has already begun. Its performance is nothing more than the further development of these initial stimuli. If we do not proceed to perform the action in spite of the felt impulse, then either the energy is not sufficient to sustain more than these first links in the mode of action from the outset, or it is checked by antithetical forces before its initial links, which are already objects of consciousness, can be translated into perceptible conduct. There are even circumstances under which the real possibility or the a priori condition of the form of behavior that is called love revives a beginning stage of its reality and brings an obscure, general feeling to consciousness, even before the supervening impulse on the part of a specific object leads it to a completed result.

Consider the fact that this diffuse—and, in a sense, invariably convoluted—urge occurs, a presentiment of the tone of love produced in a purely inward fashion, and yet still a tone of love. This is most convincing evidence for the purely inward focal nature of the phenomenon of love, which is frequently obscured by an unclear mode of thought. It is as if love were a kind of gripping or violent experience that comes from the outside (and on a subjective or metaphysical level, this can actually be the case) and has its most trenchant symbol in the "love potion"—not a mode of being and a certain modification of life as such, in which it is oriented from within to what lies outside it. It is as if love came from its object, whereas in reality it proceeds to it.

However, this immanently defined type and rhythm of the dynamic of life in which love presents itself—so that a person is loving by nature just as he is good or bad, excitable or reflective—has its polar antithesis. This is because, with the exception of religious feelings, love is more intimately and unconditionally linked with its object than any other feeling. The clearcut fashion in which love develops from the subject corresponds to the same clearcut fashion with which it is oriented to the object. The crucial point here is that no instance of a general sort is inserted between them. When I respect someone, this is mediated by what could be called his general quality of worthiness. Together with its distinctive configuration, this is permanently connected with the picture of the person as long as I respect him. The same holds for the person I fear, with whom his frightfulness and its cause are interwoven. And even as regards the person I hate, in the great majority of cases, the cause of this hate will remain in my imagination. This is one of the differences between love and hate that belies their trivial formal symmetry.[1]

And in spite of Eckhart's admonition, the total relationship of the soul to God is almost always tied to His qualities: goodness and justice, fatherliness and power. Otherwise the admonition would not have been needed. However, it is a distinctive property of love that it eliminates from its object the mediating, invariably relatively general quality that was responsible for the fact that it became an object of love. Thus love exists as an intention, directly and centrally focused on this object. It exhibits its genuine and incomparable nature precisely in those cases where it survives even the unconditional collapse of the grounds on which it developed. Eckhart's doctrine holds true only where a pure love for God is really at stake.

1. To regard love and hate as exact polar antitheses, as if it were necessary only to transpose the one into the opposite key in order to have the other, is completely mistaken. This misconception results from the fact that some externally practical consequences of the one appear to be a direct antithesis of the consequences of the other. But even this appearance is hardly exact. I wish one person good fortune and another sorrow. The presence of one person delights me, that of another is painful to me. But happiness and sorrow are not logical antitheses. Even the fact that love relatively often turns into hate proves nothing as regards their logical correlation. The opposite of love is not-love—in other words, indifference. If hate appears instead of indifference, this stems from completely new positive causes. It may be the case that these causes are secondarily connected with love; for example, the intimate relationship with the other person, the pain caused by the fact that one has deceived himself or allowed himself to be deceived, the grief due to lost opportunities for happiness, and so on.

But it holds for all love as well, because love has left behind all the attributes of the beloved that were responsible for its origin.

The ecstatic declarations of the lover—that the beloved means "the whole world to him," that "outside of her nothing exists," and similar avowals—only express this exclusiveness of love in a positive fashion. By this means, love, an utterly subjective event, embraces its object in a strict and unmediated fashion. As far as I can see, there is no other feeling with which the absolute interior of the subject penetrates the absolute character of its object so radically that, in spite of an unbridgeable opposition, the *terminus a quo* and the *terminus ad quem* coincide so unconditionally in a single stream that is not broadened at any point by an intermediate instance or case— regardless of whether such an instance may originally have been responsible for the course of the stream and may still maintain a connecting tributary channel more or less by accident.

Formally, this constellation, which includes countless gradations between transience and the most extreme intensity, is experienced in the same way in relation to a woman as to a thing, in relation to an idea as to a friend, and in relation to the fatherland as to a god. This must be settled at the outset if we want to provide a structural clarification of love's more restricted meaning, which is based on sexuality. The cavalier manner in which conventional opinion connects the sexual drive and love erects what is perhaps one of the most treacherous bridges within the psychological landscape, which already abounds with such structures. And when this view appeals to a psychology that represents itself as scientific, we might be inclined to think that psychology has fallen into the hands of journeymen butchers. On the other hand, it is obvious that the relationship should not simply be dismissed.

Our sexual dynamic moves within two strata of meaning. Behind the immediately subjective impulse and desire, consummation and the sensation of pleasure, lies the propagation of the species. Life flows in its unaccountable way along the continuity of the self-perpetuating protoplasm, either through all the stages of this continuity or conveyed by them from one point to another. Regardless of how inadequate and biased in favor of a trivial anthropomorphic symbolism the concept of means and ends may be in relation to the mysterious course of life, we must still characterize as a means that which life employs for the end of the preservation of the species. This holds true insofar as life entrusts the attainment of this end no longer to a mechanism (in the broadest sense of the word) but rather to psychic forms of mediation. There is no doubt that love springs from these forms of mediation in a continuous development. On the one hand, the typical coincidence of the period of the sexual drive with the awakening of love cannot be a mere accident; and in addition, the passionate rejection of every other sexual relationship except that with the beloved (even if this does not occur without exception) and the equally passionate yearning for this relationship would otherwise be incomprehensible.

In this case, a genetic relationship, not merely an associative relationship, must obtain. Initially the drive, in its general as well as its hedonistic sense, is oriented to the other sex as such. To the extent that its bearers have become increasingly differentiated, it seems that the drive has also increasingly individualized its object to the point of singularity. Of course there is no sense in which the drive becomes love purely as a result of its individualization. On the one hand, this process of individualization can represent a form of hedonistic refinement. On the other hand, it can be a vital-teleological instinct for the selection of the partner suited to the production of the best children. However, when the subject of this process of individualization orients it to a plurality of objects, there is no doubt that it creates a formal disposition and what might be called the space for that exclusiveness that constitutes the essence of love itself.

I have no doubt that, within what is quite generally called "sexual attraction," the initial fact or, if we like, the proto-form of love is constituted. Life is transformed into this entity as well. Its current also wells up to the level of this swell, regardless of how freely its peaks ascend. If we regard the process of life itself as a disposition of means that serve the end of life, and if we consider the purely factual significance of love for the perpetuation of the species, then love is also one of the means that life produces for itself and out of itself.

Nevertheless, at the moment that this state is attained, in which the natural development has become love with the result that love again becomes a natural development—at precisely this moment, the picture is transformed. As soon as love exists in this species—determined and teleological sense, it is also something different that transcends this status. Of course it still remains an aspect of life, but in a special way: The real dynamic of life, the process of life as naturally propelled, now exists for its sake. It signifies a meaning and a definitive state that is completely disengaged from the teleology of life. Indeed, insofar as the connection with this teleology persists, it is actually reversed: The lover feels that life now has to serve love. There is a sense in which it exists in order to provide love with the energy necessary to maintain itself. The impulsive life produces within itself points of climax in which it borders on the other order of life. At the moment of this contact, there is a sense in which these points of climax are sundered from life in order to exist in their own right and in their own sense.

Goethe's claim that everything which is complete in its own way transcends itself holds true in this case too. It is a distinctive property of life, which is always procreative in some sense or other, to bring forth more life and to be a More-Life. On the psychic level, however, it is also distinctive of life to bring forth something that is more than life and to be a More-than-Life. Live develops entities out of itself—cognitive as well as religious, aesthetic as well as social, technical as well as normative—that represent a surplus over and above the mere process of life and what stands in its service. Insofar as they form a distinctive system of logic and value that conforms to their own real content, developing into spheres that are autonomous within their own limits, they return to encounter life as contents that are enriched and intensified. However, they often have the status of ossified entities as well, in which the distinctive direction and rhythm of life are obstructed and defeated, dead ends in which life comes to a standstill.

These sequences, which may be described as "ideal," exhibit a contingency in relation to life that reaches the point of contradiction: the fact that life again realizes these "ideal" sequences in itself. Its most profound problematic lies in the consideration that these sequences as a whole have their ultimate origins in life itself and are comprehended by life. They arise out of life itself. It is the definitive nature of life to transcend itself, to create from itself what no longer qualifies as life, and to creatively confront its own course and its own conception of lawfulness with what is different from life. This transcendence, this relationship—as production, contiguity, correlation, harmony, and conflict—of the spirit to what lies beyond it but is nevertheless the form of its own inner life, is exhibited most simply in the fact of self-consciousness, the self-constitution of the subject as an object. This seems to me to be the ultimate fact of life insofar as it is spirit, and of spirit insofar as it is life. It is present not only where spiritual contents are crystallized to a point of ideal rigidity. On the contrary, even before the attainment of this aggregate state, life, while remaining quite strictly limited within itself, can generate strata both from and beyond itself in which its distinctively natural current conducive to its own ends no longer flows.

It seems to me that love resides in one of these strata. On the one hand, it is psychologically implicated in a continuously mediated and uncertain displacement from the impulse of life and its metaphysical significance. From the standpoint of its own intention, on the other hand, its immanent conception of lawfulness and its own self-development, it transcends life just as much as objectively logical knowledge transcends the psychic process of ideation, or just as much as the aesthetic value of a work of art transcends the psychological dynamics by means of which it is created or enjoyed.

Consider the problem of defining the substantial quality of love in this purely autonomous sense more positively than was done in the foregoing attempt to refute the view that love is a composite of heterogeneous elements. This problem may be insoluble. The differentiation of love from the stratum in which life itself—as sexually oriented—transpires is also quite difficult. This is because there is no sense in which love expels "sensuality" from its own stratum. I can see no basis for the claim, quite frequently heard, that eroticism and sensuality are mutually exclusive. In reality, it is love and *isolated* sensuality, the autonomy of sensual pleasure as an end in itself, that are mutually exclusive. On the one hand, this obviously fractures the unity that colors the being of the subject insofar as it loves. On the other hand, the individuality of the orientation with which love always apprehends its object, and nothing but its object, is reversed in favor of a completely non-individual pleasure, the object of which can in principle be replaced by any object at all. Since replaceability always has the character of a *means*, this object is also disclosed as nothing more than the mere means for the realization of a solipsistic purpose—which can indisputably qualify as the crassest possible antithesis to the love for this object. Moreover, it is not only the use of the person who is allegedly an object of love as a means that represents this antithesis but also the invasion of the domain of love by the teleological category as such.

In a certain sense, it is the essential characteristic of all these trans-vital realms that they remain free of the entire means-ends nexus. Just as this is precisely the meaning of Schopenhauer's remark that art "has always attained its goal," so the same holds true for love as well. Although love may also want or desire something, as long as it remains purely within itself, it never apprehends this by means of the technique of means and ends, with which all sensuality that focuses on itself alone remains bound up. On the other hand, it certainly seems to be the case—and physiological documents speak in favor of this view—that sensuality, like all other elements that are originally rooted in life itself, is taken along over the threshold of genuine love. Or, viewed from the aspect considered above, this artery also flows within the broad expanse of the homogeneous erotic stream. It is distinguished from the other arteries of this stream only retrospectively and by means of an individuating abstraction, but not in the reality of life itself. Suppose we characterize an "erotic nature" in the following way. On the one hand, the metamorphosis of the energy of life into the self-sufficient stratum of love that transcends life itself is complete. On the other hand, this stratum is vitalized and transfused by the entire unobstructed flow of the dynamic of life. In that case, there are thoroughly spiritual erotic natures, just as there are quite sensual erotic natures. The differences in psycho-physical inheritance individualize the sphere of erotics without affecting the basic indentity of its own existential decision.

What the sphere of erotics unconditionally repudiates is, of course, the interest in the perptuation of the species. The loving person as loving dissociates himself from every authentic utilitarian relationship, from the hedonistic as well as the egoistic. The moral and altruistic relationship *can* only be connected with his condition, which is always a state of being and not a state of action.[2] Similarly, a

2. The connection between love and morality, pushed to the point of identity, is just as fragile and secondary as that between religion and morality. Morality, of course, is also an "idea." It is elevated above the purposive linkages of life to a mode of being that exists purely as an end in itself and that, conversely, places all of life at its

purposive relationship to the species is alien to him as well. He is not a point of transition but rather an endpoint. Or, more correctly, his being and his sense of himself lie completely beyond the idea of path and destination and the idea of being a means and making something into a means, as also holds true for the content of religious belief and the work of art. The only difference lies in the fact that the latter are formed into enduring entities, which makes their remoteness from the teleology of life clearer than is the case for love.

This is perhaps responsible for the overtone of the tragic that we hear wafting from every great lover and every great love. It is all the more perceptible the more clearly love has detached itself from the rational process of life. It seems all the more inescapable the more love returns to life and combines with it, as in marriage. The tragedy of Romeo and Juliet lies in the *dimensions* of their love, for which the empirical world has no place. Nevertheless, because their love has its

---

disposal. Precisely for this reason, however, it will not do to legitimate religion, which falls under this same category, by means of morality, or to legitimate the former by means of the latter. And yet ultimately, this is the import of attempts to connect them. If for Kant, "the person as subordinate to moral laws" is the ultimate purpose not only of empirical human existence but even of the cosmos itself—so that religion becomes a mere appendage or, considered precisely, an instrument of morality—then this is nothing more than a falsification of the autonomous and immanently absolute nature of religion. Not only does it misconceive what seems to me to be the undeniable psychological fact that there are markedly religious persons of dubious morality and profoundly moral persons without any discernible religious impulse. In addition, it is not far from an inversion of the real substance of the matter. Granted all the trans-vitality of the idea of morality, in its genesis and functioning it is still closer to the dynamics of life and the purposes and interests of actual historical individuals and groups and more replete with them than holds true for religion. Their equivalent status as sovereign ideas stands in the way of substituting one for the other. However, if we propose to compare and connect them, then we should not overlook the difference that the more intimate teleological coupling of moral conduct implies, especially in relation to religious conduct. The view of the connection between them that makes one dependent upon the other, whether as a *ratio essendi* or as a *ratio cognoscendi*, is mistaken, both formally as well as substantively. An analogous point holds for the relationship between love and morality. There are natures of a superior ethical status for whom love—not merely in this or that sense, but in any sense—is alien. And there are erotic natures who do not even understand the nature of the moral, and still other erotic natures who, although they understand it, simply do not permit themselves to be motivated by it.

source in the empirical world and because its real development must be implicated in the contingencies of this world, it is subject to a fatal contradiction from the outset.

Suppose that tragedy does not signify simply the collision of opposed forces or ideas, desires or demands. Suppose that it lies, rather, in the fact that what a life destroys has grown out of an ultimate necessity of this life itself, that in the final analysis the tragic "conflict with the world" is a self-contradiction. In that case, all the occupants of that stratum of the "idea" are subject to tragedy. The tragic quality of what transcends the world or conflicts with it does not lie in the fact that the world cannot tolerate it, resists it, and perhaps destroys it. This would be an occasion for sorrow or out-rage. It lies, rather, in the fact that—as an idea or the incarnation of an idea—it has drawn the energy of its genesis and existence from precisely this world, in which it finds no place.

This is the basis for the tragic quality of pure eroticism which escapes from the stream of life: the fact that eroticism has its origins in this very stream, which fulfills its own most definitive law insofar as it produces something else that is alien, even antithetical, to it. The timeless beauty of Aphrodite arises out of the evanescent, wind-blown foam of the restless sea. Life, incessantly productive and incessantly prolific, has set up the attraction between the sexes as a span between two peaks of its waves. Now life undergoes that powerful axial revolution by means of which attraction becomes love: that is, ascends into the sphere of phenomena that are indiffer-ent to life and alien to all mediation and procreation. Regardless of whether this is justified by the idea or justifies the idea, regardless of whether love involuntarily assumes this retrogressive connection to life and, as reality, acquires the significance for the perpetuation of the species that I have stressed, from the standpoint of its own meaning, this interest is irrelevant to it. Love is and remains a condition of one subject which, in an inexplicable fashion that can only be experienced, embraces another subject. The focal point of love is located exclusively in itself, not in the preservation and development of the species, and not in the procreation of a third person.

On the other hand, love has its source in this life of the species, and there is some sense in which self-contradiction and self-destruction envelop love as soon as it has severed itself—as something that has its own ideal existence and autonomous meaning—from life. The tragic shadow does not fall upon love by virtue of its own properties. On the contrary, the life of the species casts this shadow. From its own energies and in the interest of the expediencies of its own development, the life of the species thrusts itself upward until it blossoms as love. However, at the moment that the blossoms of love open, they send their fragrance aloft into a realm of freedom beyond the soil in which they are rooted. It is not, of course, destruction and a fatal outcome that are tragic. On the contrary, it is the contradiction: the fact that beside or above life, which attempts to embrace everything, an alien entity is juxtaposed to it, cut off from its creative stream and drawing happiness and misery from its own origins; that this very entity has its origins in a most profound intention or necessity—or, perhaps more correctly, in a norm—of this life; that this estrangement from life is its own ultimate mystery. This self-negation, even if it is not an aggressive negation of life, is responsible for the hushed tragic music that intones before the door of love.

Perhaps tragedy already lies in the pure autonomy of love. This is because there is a contradiction between the irredeemable immanence of emotion in its bearer and the embrace of the other, between withdrawal into the self and the desire for fusion, a contradiction in the process between the I and the Thou, which even this ultimate instance cannot secure from continual resumption. In this context, however, we are concerned with a different sort of tragedy, in which the threat to love comes from the life of the species. In love, this life has transcended itself. Out of its own energies, it has given birth to what is unfaithful to life. It has produced a stratum that may still be embraced by its cosmic-metaphysical meaning. This is because, in the light of this meaning, life itself is more "than" life. Nevertheless, in this stratum life has deserted its own law of being more-life.

The diverse relationships in which individuality and the life of the species are interwoven in love are extremely complicated and finely intermeshed. However, there is no sense in which the complication always lies in experience itself. On the contrary, experience is quite often completely monochromatic and in itself unrefracted. Only a refractive reproduction, for which our concepts are not sufficiently sophisticated, compounds experience out of elements that are variously fractured, diametrically juxtaposed to one another, and only partially interwoven. Consider the fact that the distinctive structure of concepts resists analysis into small parts which would conform to one another in a continuous fashion so that at least a symbolically adequate facsimile of the unity of experience would be produced. At least in part, this can be ascribed to the fact that philosophy has ignored the erotic problem. Aside from individual exceptions, the discussions in the *Phaedrus* and the *Symposium* and the extremely one-sided reflections of Schopenhauer are all that the great thinkers have contributed to this problem. As a result, even the concepts that are useful in any way at all have remained rigid, undifferentiated, and without a real possibility of more precise formulation. Given this proviso, therefore, it seems to me that the individualism of love is one of its essential determinants. I will elucidate what I have in mind here with two of Goethe's couples.

The fact that, from a distance, Faust and Gretchen are regarded as the erotic ideal type is proof of how seldom the idea of love rises above its purely general character. There is no doubt that for Faust experience as a whole is defined by the incomparable individuality of his own inner fate. Within the psychically metaphysical development, the externalities of what happens to him are nothing more than a symbol. However, precisely because they only have to fulfill a specific function within an immeasurable process, as an erotic event they are intrinsically of a thoroughly unindividual nature. Gretchen certainly does not love Faust as a personality, but rather as the spiritual, utterly towering and domineering man. It is one of thousands of relationships in which a girl of noble character and an inferior level of culture is filled with a diffuse, perhaps unconscious yearning for a more sublime world, not a glimmer of which penetrates the circumstances of her own life. She falls victim to a man who descends to her from that world, bringing unimagined fulfillments and dazzling her unaccustomed eyes with its sun. Here resistance is no more possible than it was for the daughters of the earth against Zeus. In the same way that this kind of man can seduce any number of girls of this sort, the surrender of the girl is not tied to the singular nature of the man at all but only to his type.

Gretchen knows nothing of the uniqueness of Faust's personality. She probably does not even suspect it. In any case, she is not in love with it. When she speaks of Faust in her monologues, the language is remarkably lacking in individuality. For her, Faust is "this sort of man." However, that this general image is worthy of the entire intensity of her emotions and the commitment of her entire existence is based on the fact that for women as such, the general—sexual life as a whole, the relationship to children, the activities and emotions that define the sphere of the home and the family—easily becomes a thoroughly individual experience. Because of their ostensibly or actually more profound emotional depths they intensify what the man accepts as something general and typical, to the point that it becomes a matter of purely individual fate and the ultimate focus of the personality.

For Faust himself, experience is simply an adventure. In conformity with his nature, the unity of which is a consequence of the polar elements of reflection and the ease with which he is unnerved, his experience, of course, deepens and entangles him. However the character of the adventure remains. And the rather superficial manner in which he conceives the woman's nature corresponds to what might be called the determination to fill a schematically pre-figured place in the program of his life. Consider the typically masculine attitude in his relationship with a woman. Ultimately the man thinks about himself, not about the woman. This holds true even when he blows his brains out on her account. In fact, it holds true especially in this case. Here, of course, this attitude has a more profound justification: The experience is only a symbol, only an unavoidable station along his immense journey. However, this does not alter the fact that, in his immanently erotic character, Faust takes in Gretchen merely as a general being. On the contrary, it only makes this fact clear. It is "the passion for her sweet *body*" that drives him to her. Moreover, it is no less alien to individuality because 'body', in this context, may have a significance that goes beyond anatomy. Faust gives no indication that he has any sense at all of what is most profoundly characteristic of her own passion: its grand *heroism*, exercised in few words and with little consciousness.

Ultimately, everything enchanting and moving in this erotic relationship is barely able to conceal the fact that each lover neglects precisely the most individual qualities of the beloved. I would like to venture the undemonstrable speculation that Goethe subsequently realized this himself. Only retrospectively, in Gretchen's transfigured reappearance, did he underpin this relationship with a transcendent depth. There is a sense in which he legitimated it metaphysically by the subsequent marriage in Heaven. However, this does not change the original nature of the relationship at all. On the contrary, it only underscores it all the more. This is because the real force of the reappearance of Gretchen lies in the *eternally* feminine: in other words the timeless and purely trans-individual feminine. But this final elevation of the relationship—which also signifies the ultimate depth it attains—is only the metaphysical sublimation of its nature as a thoroughly general entity. Nevertheless, there is no sense in which it follows that the relationship remains incorporated within the intra-erotic life of the species. Rather, it proves to be a fully enfranchised inhabitant of the territory of genuine love.

But this does not yet identify what we may call absolute love. It conforms to this designation only if everything related to the species is refined out and the feeling holds exclusively for the irreplaceable personality as such. And as regards what concerns the species, there is no sense in which this is limited to the purely sensual. On the contrary, as in the case of Gretchen's love, it can include whatever has spiritual and general human significance. For the relationship between Eduard and Ottilie, the complete antithesis to Faust and Gretchen, this is crucial. As regards the nature of the love between Faust and Gretchen, the possibility of replaceability is by no means inconceivable. This holds true regardless of the extent to which Gretchen—conforming to that female emotional individualization of what concerns the species—unalterably binds her passion to this single representative of values which are basically quite definitely not individual. In the case of Eduard and Ottilie, however, Goethe has succeeded—as in none of his other love stories—in producing the impression that here all replaceability is a priori excluded, in the most precise sense of this term. (Of course this holds true for Charlotte and the captain as well, as Goethe indicates by placing them under the same concept of elective affinity. However, it holds to a more limited degree. Again, this shows in a very interesting way that the types of love, which in essence are unconditionally distinct from one another, always leave space for the most diversified gradations.) It is only in the case of Eduard and Ottilie that passion is exhaustively determined by the fate of individuality. Individuality obviously presupposes sexual differentiation as a law of the species. Eduard and Ottilie must be man and woman. Sexuality as a total coloration of the individual, but not as an autonomous entity abstracted from love itself, is decisive for such an absolute love. Neither lover has a heart that throbs for sexuality as something purely general. In the case of the erotic, and in other cases as well, continuity, which cannot be separated from the life of the species, is shattered against absolute individuality.

For Faust, Gretchen is first of all just a girl, an exemplar of Everywoman, for Faust is determined to see Helen in every woman. Moreover, Gretchen is a girl endowed with the qualities of Everywoman intensified to the extent that the threshold of erotic excitement is crossed: *genus plus differentia specifica*. Eduard's passion, on the other hand, is focused on Ottilie's absolute individuality, which is, of course, thoroughly feminine. But in it that ideal line of demarcation is completely erased, with the result that it becomes impossible to link this passion to any other specific type of passion, perhaps through the basis of the general as a medium. Eduard and Ottilie love one another because it is written in the stars. Faust and Gretchen love one another only because they have met.

Nothing depicts the difference better than the transcendent presentiments that decide the fate of each of these characters. Gretchen is a penitant, the radiance of that eternally feminine that is decisive here, the symbol of a mystery that lies completely beyond the individual. However, it is the "heartfelt moment when someday they will awaken together" that awaits Eduard and Ottilie. The endless future is limited to the two of them and their "union." But this does not mean that something arises beside them or above and beyond them whose celestial radiance would obscure the contours of their absolute individuality.

Thus I believe I may designate as absolute that love in which the elimination of everything concerning the species and the a priori exclusion of any replaceability of the individual are only two expressions of exactly the same attitude. In this case, the pure concept of love, the extension of one subject to the other which is wrenched from every aspect of the life of the species and remains completely within the subject as a thoroughly individual feeling, achieves its rare and consummate realization. Therefore I can describe as an a priori only the certainty with which it places every mistaken conflation beyond discussion. It should not be confused with those cases in which, *after* the choice is made and the possible relationship to the entire sex is concentrated on a single individual, there can no longer be any question of another person. This is an a posteriori exclusiveness. It holds true for the future. In the case of absolute love, however, exclusiveness ideally holds for the past as well. There are marvelous cases of love that completely exhibit the phenomenon of the absolute. In the sense of a posteriori exclusiveness, however, they are only empirical. They are related to the absolute in the same way that the infinity of time is related to atemporality. It could be said that practically there is no difference between them either.

The love of Eduard and Ottilie presupposes the differentiation of the sexes. This is, of course, only the all-pervasive coloration of the total individuality and the exclusive subject and object of this love. It forms a distinctive element of love only for a retrospective and imaginary abstraction. In the same way, the most genuine love, even in its sublimation to the absolute, provides no resistance at all to the entry desired by sensuality and its consequences for the preservation of the species, no more than it resists a destiny that is connected with the personality at its center. It is only that, in light of its meaning, such a love is related to the life of the species and its purposes as objective facts, in the same way that it is related to something alien and indifferent.

I have considered the tragic quality of love, which makes its opposition to the life of the species felt as a resistance against the undeniable genesis of love in the species. This issue is probably not merely a matter of the genesis of the erotic but of its permanent *foundation* as well. That is because the radical character of the opposition by means of which I have attempted to define the nature of the erotic holds true only as a principle or an idea. Neither in phylogenetic nor in ontogenetic reality does this radical opposition represent a historically unique break. Even the question of whether this break ever really occurs in the phenomenal world remains uncertain. In this domain of life, it is rather the case that genuine trans-vital love continually arises from the life of the species and in conformity with it, in either a fragmentary or a complete fashion;

sometimes as a mere longing; sometimes as a vault upward that quickly sinks back into life; in some cases with a relatively stable compromise or a compounding of the biological with the purely erotic; and on other occasions with the unstable and varying dominance of the parties.

In any case, once the contradiction between them appears, it implies not only the tragedy discussed above but also a threat to the species life that is quite real. With the increasingly intensive development of the erotic, the pure individual—in other words, the central or total subject—is instituted and advanced. As I have said, it is not the case that biologically defined and species-relevant determinations are eliminated. Nevertheless, from a disjunctive standpoint, now they qualify as nothing more than one of many factors that seem to synthesize a personality. Among these factors, those which are remote from the immediate life of the species—for reasons that are comprehensible, even though they may be only transitory—receive the most conscious emphasis.

However, this can have dangerous consequences for the preservation of the species. As long as interest in the preservation of the species dominates the existence—even if not the consciousness—of mankind, love, at least on the part of the woman, can be regarded as the instinct or the standard-bearer of the instinct for the father of the best possible child. Herein lies the biological justification for the love match. No such justification is needed as long as the human material is assumed to be relatively undifferentiated. Within such a population, the question of which pair is joined is more or less irrelevant for the quality of the next generation. It is obvious that the interest in this quality acquires a practical significance only where personalities are powerfully individualized. It is only from this standpoint that the choice of a spouse can become right or wrong.

Suppose that a compulsory institution made it possible to bring the most fit specimens together. Even so, it is well known that in the case of highly differentiated and extremely complex beings, we have no way of identifying this quality of fitness with any certainty; in the area of animal husbandry, of course, a swift inspection by the expert is all that is required for this purpose. Here it is only instinct, and not warranted knowledge, that stands at the disposal of species fitness. The selection of the biologically appropriate partner may be ascribed and entrusted to the conscious form of this instinct as individually erotic attachment.

The popular belief in the exceptional excellence of "children of love" can be based only on the following consideration; Love develops precisely where the individual parents are determined to produce the best child together. Consider our account according to which love as such wrenches itself from the stream of life of species fitness in order to constitute a mode of being of the subject with its own center. In itself, that account is not inconsistent with this popular belief. This is because the genesis of love lies in this stream of life, which it transcended only to gain its own autonomy. Beyond this limit, it at once takes on contents and colorations, impulses and values that have developed in its vital form and now are only reborn in a new key and with a new centrality, comparable to the naturalistic perception of things in the work of art.

However, to the extent that love also draws its meaning from the total cosmos of the personality, a departure from this remnant of species fitness is threatened by precisely this subjective centrality. On the one hand, this meaning becomes increasingly rich in diverse elements. On the other hand, it becomes more highly individualized and, in a certain sense, more endowed with its own autonomous will. For now, this new and authentic love is also fed by all those elements that lie outside the domain of what is vital to the species. Moreover, in their tendency and character, it is these elements that may very well prove to be paramount. Empirical considerations seem to establish this as a matter of fact. At least in our upper classes, we can observe that the love of women, and to a lesser extent that of men as well, is increasingly tied to the *spiritual* qualities of the partner and less frequently to the instinct for the partner's biological fitness, even though there is no sense in which this is invariably the case. Beginning insignificantly and thwarted and counteracted in a thousand different ways, one of the most colossal developments imaginable is introduced by this development: Its progress deprives us of our only index of the biological adequacy of acts of procreation, and the love match loses its biological value!

With this vital contradiction, there is a sense in which the tragedy of the erotic fact would constitute itself as a body. Consider the process by which love becomes autonomous in relation to life, which creates love for its own "purposes"; the concentration of love in the constitution of its bearer, its extension to his trans-biological energies, and the process by which it becomes absolutized in the irreplaceable character of his individuality. Initially, all this is only linked with the *indifference* of love to the teleology of the species life. It confirms the axiom of life; to thrust forward what transcends life, with its absolute distinctive reality and its own conception of lawfulness, according to the law that this life does not merely continue on its own level but rather passes into the dimension that lies above it.

At this point, however, mere indifference threatens to develop into positive antagonism. These determinations of love seem gradually to deprive it of the meaning and bliss with which it had reached back into life from the domain of its trans-vital autonomy. If this development persists, then it would seem to be increasingly clear that it represents the destiny of life: to pull down in its wake the bridges it has built for its own passage and to acknowledge this demolition itself as its most immanent necessity, as the ultimate fulfillment of its law of self-transcendence.

I have stressed the point that the concept of love covers an extremely broad concept of the relationship between the I and the world. The nature of the specifically erotic as well is clarified by virtue of the fact that there are innumerable areas in which feelings, which certainly do not bear the name of love as a consequence of arbitrary misunderstandings or misusage, extend beyond all sexuality. Consider the idea that love, although generated by procreative beings, nevertheless ascends into a new category which is indifferent to that life at the moment when it becomes purely autonomous. This idea is all the more persuasive when love falls under this category together with other "loves" that have a different content and origin. And this conviction is not diminished but rather strengthened if the formal development is shown to be parallel to the sexual. Here too we can see that in many cases the causal and functional aspects of life as primary and as biologically, egoistically, and socio-religiously defined produce emotional relationships that have the nature of love. However, these relationships do not remain submerged in the stream of this life. On the contrary, they ascend into that trans-vital realm that can be called ideal, in the most comprehensive and nontheoretical sense. This ascent is identical with what happens when the event develops from an instrumentally purposive state, interwoven with action, and in some way or other external to that inner and central state of the subject, the only state that can really be called love. In this context, two groups of phenomena are of the most universal importance. In light of their most manifest clearcut cases, I shall designate them as universal philanthropy and Christian love.

What we typically conceive as universal philanthropy is defined by the consideration that the feeling of love is no longer focused upon the individual because of his individual mode of existence. As the erotic, of course, it never pertains to this or that single quality of the beloved. At most, such a quality forms the medium in consciousness for the relationship to the total picture of the person, the real object of the erotic, which resists any localization in specifiable qualities. However, the individualism of love is demonstrated precisely by the fact that a basis in these qualities is repudiated. Every "quality" is general and can attach to an indefinite number of subjects. But that truly individual and irreducibly integral total which qualifies as love lies beyond all qualities. It is situated in a nexus of these qualities, which does not lie in the qualities themselves.

At this point, however, we are concerned with a kind of love that abstracts from this individual uniqueness. It rather receives its orientation from the fact that it applies to everything that bears a human face. It is different from the cosmic eros, the pantheism of love, the universal love that flows from the subject through the world, as if in a total mass. That is because, in these cases, the a priori is the *life* of the personality; for this reason, it is just as continuous as life itself. This sort of love is bestowed upon God and the worm, the star and the plant, upon everything real simply because it is real: in other words, an object of precisely this subject. This uninterrupted love is expressed either as a general mood of delicate lyricism, or as a religious devotion to all things because they are of God or nature, or as a genuinely rational consistency, which is more an idea and a requirement than an emotional experience—and naturally it always incorporates human beings into its unlimited domain.

"Universal philanthropy," on the other hand, has a different nature. It is not part of a more comprehensive absolute. On the contrary, it only infuses that special relationship that obtains between one person and another precisely insofar as they are persons. Moreover, this tends to occur with a certain exclusiveness that makes its bearers more remote from that pantheistic love. It seems relatively certain that universal philanthropy, precisely as an emotional state of love, is in general quite dispassionate. It has something of the abstract character of all the generalities that the eighteenth century made into value concepts: the general rights of man, the general moral law of the Kantian ethic, and the general humanistic religious idea of deism. In this form, universal philanthropy is really concerned with the person as an abstraction. Because it applies to the concrete individual only indirectly and through the medium of this abstraction, it has often lost so much of its ardor that it signifies little more than a qualification of the view of man as *homo homini lupus*. Nevertheless, a phenomenon of love is present even in this attenuated state. Like the erotic on the grand scale, it has divested itself of its original, purely existential nexus.

I have no doubt that universal philanthropy has its basis or protoform in those cordial and often genuinely affectionate sentiments that inescapably arise within practical-social relationships, of both a more intimate and a more remote sort. They are inescapable because there are no utilitarian considerations, no external compulsion, and no ethic of any sort that could maintain the stability and existential function of this kind of cohesiveness if social sentiments—that people are well disposed toward one another and are *content* in their relationships—were not dispersed between the strands of the relations woven by those rational forces. If the view of man as *homo homini lupus* were really true—a position that should not, of course, be rejected on the basis of a cheerful moral optimism—then we would find that an abiding and intimate social life with persons toward whom we had this disposition would simply exceed the limits of what we could tolerate psychically. By itself, law, regardless of how precise and rigorous its execution, could never hold a society together if it were not complemented by morally voluntary acts of goodness and decency, harmony and good will. In the same way, even these voluntary acts together with the law would still not result in a possible society if they were not also complemented by those emotional propensities and that affection and sympathy without which sociological proximity and intimacy and constant mutual contact would be utterly unbearable.

Congenial neighborly sentiments, even granting that we harbor no illusions about their reliability, extent, and depth, are still an indispensable cement for every group, perhaps less in the sense that they establish positive ties than in the following: Without them, a socialized state of existence—namely, one in which personalities are already differentiated—would inevitably become a hell. Friendly and cordial sentiments between persons in a relationship of close proximity tend not to be the cause of this relationship. It is rather that the sentiment is only a consequence of this relationship, which has been brought about by some cause or other. Moreover this does not happen—as a completely unilluminating platitude has it—as a result of the "habit" of social life. It is rather the case that a continuous social life and even habituation to it would be impossible if that sentiment of moderation did not develop relatively quickly between the parties within this social life as a kind of organic precautionary measure against its difficulties and abrasions. In other words, if the forms and force vectors of societies in general arise as necessities of an instrumentally purposive process of life, then these affectionate or quasi-erotic feelings have the same social-teleological genesis. They are implicated in the praxis of social life, just as the primary sexual drives are implicated in the praxis of sexual life. And just as genuine love arises from the latter emotional state by means of a total revolution of meaning, so it seems that universal philanthropy owes its existence to those vital and societal feelings. Naturally this does not take place in a mechanical parallel with the individualistic erotic phenomenon, but rather with modifications and reductions in intensity that are quite significant. However, the fundamental form is the same.

The interpretation of universal philanthropy as nothing more than the gradual extension of these elements of societal life would amount to the most banal sort of associationistic psychology. In its pure form, it has rather broken in its wake the bridges to every teleology. It is a pure turning of the feeling into itself that is alien to praxis. Of course it can also be turned back into life and expressed in actions. It is an immanent disposition of the subject, not with respect to another specific person or plurality of persons, but rather with respect to the human type in general, regardless of where it is realized in the individual.[3]

There is a profound function that has a formally psychic status and that can only be characterized as an abstraction: the concentration or channeling of an energy of consciousness onto certain elements of its object. Although the other elements of the object form a *substantial* unity with them, now the light of consciousness does not shine upon these other elements. This is due not to the accidental fact that no notice is taken of them but, rather, to the fact that psychic energy has an affinity only with the former elements. As a result, it forms them into a new substantial unity that now represents the totality of the object.

This function can become operative in all possible areas of intellectuality as well as inner religious ferment, in feeling as well as formative power. Occasionally it may also betray an intellectualistic character within the feeling now under discussion. However, that signifies an attenuation and artificiality of the feeling. In its pure form, this is an entity that is entirely *sui generis*. The fact that it is focused not upon specific individuals but rather upon all individuals is the clearest index of its detachment from a practically vital linkage and of its nature as a pure state of the subject. Without sociality and its emotional contingencies, however, the genesis of this feeling is just as improbable as that of eroticism without sexuality. This feeling, which has already become trans-singular within the domain of social life, is now completely drawn into the subject, from which it flows once more as if from its original source. In that proto-form, however, it was nothing more than a ripple that the continuity of the stream of life of society had cast and then taken back into itself once more.

This metamorphosis in a disposition of the subject is to be expected only within what might be called its completely diffuse, and thus uncircumscribed, activity. Consider the fact that it breaks away

---

3. Again, love for the "human being" as an idea, love for the race as a value that stands above individuals, is something entirely different. Psychologically, it is often utterly incompatible with philanthropy. Nietzsche possessed and preached love for the human being in this sense with a most passionate intensity. However, he completely rejected universal philanthropy in his doctrine and probably in his personal feelings as well.

from its social proto-forms very rarely and also quite late historically. That is no proof against this connection, no more than it speaks against our interpretation of love that the net gains it achieves from its own sexually vital proto-form may occur late and in any case infrequently. Regardless of how superficial and unilluminating this love for every person as such may appear when compared with the erotic, it is still based on the same fundamental reversal. In relation to the centrality of the sociological life, the social proto-forms of this sort of love are subordinate and instrumental. On the other hand, where universal philanthropy is emotionally and existentially genuine, it is lodged within the center of the subject. It is a self-sustaining, self-sufficient value, not bound to any purpose that generates it. On the contrary, it steadily emits a warm, soft luster from itself alone.

It is the elimination of the individual differences of its objects that gives the feeling of universal philanthropy the character of an abstraction. While it is clear that this already occurs to a certain extent in the case of gregariousness, universal philanthropy continues it to the point where it becomes unconditional. This is possible as a result of the fact that the emotional state disengages itself from the attachment to life. It no longer finds its point of departure in individual realities. On the contrary, it moves within that distinctive unity of subjective centrality and idea which constitutes the nature of genuine erotic love as well, and which now projects itself outward into the "generality" and homogeneity of its objects.

Compared with this abstractive character of universal philanthropy, what we call Christian love is a kindred phenomenon, and yet also quite different. In Christian love, the individual person is not loved because of what he has in common with everyone else; in other words, that which disregards his own distinctive and personal qualities in principle, or includes them only because they exist in a personal union with his general qualities. Christian love rather embraces the *total* person. Its distinctive character lies in the fact that, although it is focused upon absolutely every person, it is wholly indifferent to the question of whether or not one person has something in common with another. We are loved just as we are, from the periphery to the center. The definitive consideration is perhaps the following. Although the sinner is also an object of universal philanthropy, this is really *in spite of* the fact that he is a sinner, and only because, ultimately, he is a human being as well. Christian love, on the other hand, embraces the sinner—and precisely as a sinner—if not with a greater love than is bestowed upon the normal person, then at least without that "in spite of."

Consider the incomparable quality of the love which, in light of its historical situation, we are obliged to call "Christian"—even though its decisive structure is more evident on the basis of the interpretation of certain sayings of Jesus and the psychology of their praxis than from what has been established as a dogmatic or literary canon. It lies in this relationship to the principle of individuality. On the one hand, it holds true for the individual *as if* it held for his total and personal nature, becoming absorbed in him as a distinctive individual. On the other hand, there is no sense in which its motive is the comparable or incomparable individuality of the other person. The definitive characteristic of this structure lies in the fact that the alternative between individuality and generality as a motive proves to be inadequate. It is a fundamental, emotive embrace of *all* individualities, and yet it does not take place under the auspices of the concept of universality. This occurs only where Christian love limits itself to fellow believers.

However, it seems to me that this is not the meaning of its ultimate depth. If Saint Francis loves the birds and the fishes, then this is, of course, an outgrowth of his absolutely loving, compulsively loving, nature. Nevertheless, it occurs in a direction that was given with the Christian temper, and to a degree or an extent that outstrips what would otherwise be its given energy. The decisive feature of Christianity lies precisely in the fact that it defines the soul in an a priori fashion as loving. As a result, its love must be all-embracing, even if the dynamic in this case usually does not extend beyond all humanity.

Naturally, no one who is not intrinsically erotic can acquire an erotic nature from Christianity. The difference remains that in one with the erotic nature, one who is loving on the basis of the ultimate ground of his nature, love follows the rhythm and the fluctuations of the process of life. Thus in spite of its continuous scope and its power to define all possible relationships to other persons, love in principle implies no *equivalence* of these relationships, no sentiment that would be a priori immune to the influence of individual dispositions.

Consider the erotic nature in its most consummate sense. It is a life with an intention that is obedient only to itself and defined exclusively from within. That is why even this nature exhibits the differences in accent, the up and down quality, the trans-mechanical and—in a certain sense—capricious quality that constitute the nature of life as such. This holds true in relation to all the contingencies that it can experience in any fashion from the outside. It also holds true in relation to any forces whatsoever; although they may not qualify as concepts themselves, they can still be expressed as concepts and as entities that have an autonomous existence. Where life is derived from such a nature, it can acquire from this nature a uniformity of its moments in relation to which its natural self-formative activity has something arbitrary about it. It exhibits conformity to a law, but not conformity to a rule.

This differentiates the distinctive nature of Christian love from the other two forms, which in principle also extend to everything that bears a human face. Universal philanthropy is differentiated from Christian love by virtue of the fact that it grasps only the typical aspects of the human being as such. The totality of the differentiated person is ignored, or at least it is included only in this indirect fashion. Although the erotic nature is utterly indifferent to this sort of generality and although, like Christian love, it draws individuality completely into its sphere, it does so with a multiplicity of different emphases and intensities. This is because the erotic nature stems quite directly from life as primary and individual as well, concomitant with its rhythmic and arhythmic course. Christian love, on the other hand, is governed by an idea that lies beyond life; the common Fatherhood of God, the commandments of Jesus, or love for God, of which Christian love is a contingent product or substitute. This is precisely why, consistent with its own principle, it cannot make the distinction among persons that is made by life; and why, although it is concerned with the individualities of persons, it can ground no difference in its acts of love on their differences.

The lack of differentiation characteristic of Christian love is also supported by two other considerations. It is connected with the absolute value of the human soul. I am well aware that objections can be raised against this absolutist interpretation of "equality before God": As regards their ethical value, differences among souls were overlooked neither by Jesus himself nor by the authorities of Christendom; the equivalence of their metaphysical value is directly contradicted by the doctrine of predestination; and even in the state of everlasting bliss, the gradation leading down from the major saints completely invalidates the absolute character of the value of the soul, which would not permit this sort of relativity. Nevertheless, I am convinced that there is a sense in which none of these differences touches the foundation of the matter; rather, they arise on the basis of an absolute value that is presupposed. Predestination directly signifies indifference to *every* autonomous human value. It sets the divine will, the only source of value, above every such absolute or relative value. On the basis of its own premises, therefore, predestination cannot be the decisive factor in this context. Or, considering the matter positively, from the standpoint of religious ethics it is quite obvious that the *eternal* torments of hell can be justified only by the negation or perversion of an *absolute* value. In that case, I cannot see why such a value should not be exhibited by different natures in different degrees. Otherwise the differences in intensity of the torments of hell, which in their extent are equally absolute, would be unintelligible.

Suppose that gold qualified as the absolute economic value. Nevertheless, there are still larger or smaller gold pieces, and those which are more or less alloyed. Each functions as a uniform quantum of value, and yet each also makes diverse degrees of the absolute value possible, just as the absolute value of the soul is graduated in the levels of paradise. Moreover, it is inconceivable that God should have offered love to *all* men if the gradation of value—from the highest positive value to the lowest negative value—had not left an absolute core of value that is present *everywhere* untouched. And even the mere *possibility* of aspiring to the realization of the highest level of value signifies that the soul has a metaphysical value which is already absolute, regardless of the relative phenomenon in which it is psychologically developed by the soul. Although it is certainly true that heights and depths, good and evil, and stupidity and enlightenment are of considerable importance for all possible interests of Christianity, they do not have this status precisely in regard to the love that is vouchsafed everyone.

This general and invariable requirement would not be comprehensible as such if it were based on a structure of value defined by that relativity. It can only be based on a value of the soul itself, a value that is intrinsically absolute. In this case, of course, love— which can still adduce the authority of its own immanent *ratio*—does not yet exist on its highest level. This level would be reached only if that ultimate fundamental value—and thus every quality that it justifies—had also vanished, only if vileness, evil, and insensibility were the definitive nature of every man, without sparing even a glimmer of value—and yet love still appeared. Only then would love really qualify as a *causa sui*, only then would there be love for the sake of love and not in the interest of some motive that lies outside love itself. Christian love would advance beyond itself, even if in its own direction.

However, this consideration as well, the fact that it does not hold true for Christian love, that it is tied to a faith in the absolute value of the soul as the a priori destination point of the movement of love— this faith, which is of course deeply religious, like the belief in the absolute value of existence in general, even if the "world" is execrable, wretched, and godforsaken—is sufficient to provide the positive underpinning for the undifferentiated state of Christian love. Thus it is established that Christian love is not concerned with personal differences, which can only be relative in comparison with the absolute value of the soul. As a result, however, this love places itself beyond life, which inevitably transpires in relativities and judgments concerning the nature and value of persons and, in conformity with these judgments, in the differential reactions of our sensibility and conduct.

Finally, a third point concerning this same result stems from the behavior of the lover himself. This behavior follows a type, the form of which is defined especially clearly in the ethics of Kant. Kant perceived the fundamental mutual estrangement, even heterogeneity, of the two elements of the moral world in a completely categorical fashion: freedom and the law. He unified them with the explanation that genuine freedom consists in fulfilling the law. In dealing with the problem of two religious demands that run in parallel or opposed directions, the individual salvation of the soul and love, Christianity proceeds in accordance with this view. It escapes a dualism of these demands with the stipulation that love is the path to salvation. But even if they are considered from the standpoint of the motive of attaining salvation, the objects of the acts of love have no differentia that could claim to distinguish these acts from one another on the basis of their own significance.

Of course Christian love—because it completely penetrates the individuality of its object and submits to it, even though the *differentiated* character of this individuality does not concern it—escapes the questionable consequences of the following fact: In the lack of importance of the value and dignity of the object for the act of love itself, there is a certain contemptuousness. This is an excessively sharp accentuation of a feature of all love: It is undeserved. Even the same mutual love cannot simply be reckoned so that no unpaid balance remains. Love belongs among the quantitatively indeterminable values, those values which, in principle, are not to be "earned." This is why we cannot really have a "claim" to love either. On the contrary, under all conditions, even where the most exalted liberality and equivalent values compel it and seem to give us a right to love, it still remains a gift and a blessing.

Nevertheless, everything unearned that we receive from another person is somehow oppressive, even if it is a blessing and a delight. And even though it may seem humiliating only to a false pride, the more free and expansive thinker also feels humbled in response to it. The acceptance of every great love contains an element of this humility. However, we can be more or less "worthy," even of a "blessing." Precisely insofar as it is love, this difference does not exist for Christian love, even though it may insert this difference into other sequences of value. This fact could easily lead to a feeling of humiliation, especially if the undeserved blessing not only is a gift of free grace but is also bestowed equally on every being.

This feeling can be suppressed only by the interest in the complete individuality of its object that exists for this form of love. However, estrangement from the form of life as such persists here as well, where the personal motive in achieving one's own salvation through love brings Christian love especially close to life, with its natural and primary drives. This is because these drives—the less they are channeled by ideas or norms—completely follow the contingencies of inner development or external impulses. Regardless of the extent to which the life of the ego in itself may conform to law, and regardless of the extent to which all its expressions may acquire a common coloration as a result of its steadfast fundamental character, in a certain sense its relationship to the world—precisely when this life is subject to the unity that lies within it alone—is capricious, thoroughly distinctive, sometimes resting on this point, sometimes on that as the goal of its impulses.

There is no doubt that the religious life itself leads immanently to the attitude of love, even if in the most diverse stages and modes. If for no other reason, this holds true because the idea of every divine being represents a focal point on which the existential radiance of many individuals, together with that of the individual believer, is concentrated. I know of no religion that fails to include some sort of metaphysical, ritual, or practical solidarity and some sort of altruistic injunction, even if only within a quite restricted sphere. Quite often, religion is even the expression or the hypostatization for the uniformity of a group. The more religion appears as an aspect of the vital dynamic of life, the more certainly will inter-individual consequences follow from it, as if they were determined by love for the fellow believers for whom they are intended, even if in fact other motives are responsible for this.

If its nature is transposed from a mode of the conduct of life into a dogma, then this result becomes more problematic. That is because in dogma, the removal of religion from the sphere of life and its shift into the sphere of the idea are complete. Christian dogma, on the other hand, has incorporated love into itself and thereby elevated it into this second sphere. As "Christian love," it can exhibit in this sphere that distinctive form of universality with which it discloses to us its estrangement from the characteristic rhythm of life as such. Insofar as Christianity is regarded as religious life in an unspecific sense, it leads only to the threshold of love, in the same way that this holds true for sexuality in *its* domain. To this extent, love is only latent in Christianity, a by-product of the general focus of the religious life.

At this point, however, Christianity produces the great axial revolution. In a reversal, love becomes an ultimate central point—as a result of which it really becomes "love" for the first time—and life with its religious energies is summoned for the realization of this point. Subsequently, of course, it can react upon life and be assimilated into it. In that case, however, it remains an assimilated content that stems from a sphere of its own validity, not from life itself.

There is no sense in which life itself decides the distinctive form of love. The proto-form of love is indeed an element or a product of the religious life, just as it is an element or product of biological life. But when it really becomes Christian love and a constituent of dogma, it also transcends this mode or domain of the dynamic of life. Once again incorporated into life, it discloses its trans-vital nature by virtue of the fact that it frees itself from the selective and individualistic determinations of life as such, its discontinuities, limits, and suscep-tibilities, and those of the religious life as well.

INDEX

Acting: female contribution to, 85–87, 89–90

Beauty: and the nature of women, 87–89
Bebel, August, 33–35
Broch, Hermann, 19n

Culture: nature of, 6, 9, 55; reification of, 9–13; feminization of, 25, 54
—objective: explained, 6–11, 65–66; and the division of labor, 19–22, 69–70; feminist politics of, 26n, 43–44, 54–55; and the women's movement, 66–67; masculine character of, 67–69, 74–75, 95–97; prospects for the feminization of, 98–99; consistency with the female nature, 99–101
—subjective: explained, 7–11, 65–66; and the division of labor, 19–22; and the women's movement, 66, 75–76
—instrumentalization of: explained, 9, 13–14, 19; and the problem of the meaning of life, 14–15; and modernity, 15–16; role of money as the paradigm of, 17–18
—and women: separate spheres model of, 26–30, 35; liberal model of, 30–32, 35–36; socialist model of, 32–35; Simmel's conception of, 40–45. *See also* Division of labor; Forms; Life; Objectification

Dilthey, Wilhelm, 3, 56
Division of labor: male character of, 70, 105–06; resistance of women to, 70–71. *See also* Culture; Objectification

Eckhart, Johannes (Meister), 161, 164

Feminism: problem of in Simmel's work, 25–26; and objective culture, 25–26; and subjective culture, 25–26; and politics of culture, 26n; liberal, 31, 35–36n, 44; socialist, 35–36n, 44. *See also* Culture; Women
Flirtation: conduct typical of, 134–35; nature of, 134–52, passim; and uncertainty, 136, 143–44, 151; and adornment, 136–38; and intellectuality, 138; and the female nature, 138–42, 147–49; and power, 141; relation to art, 144–47; relation to play, 150–52; as a form, 150–52; and the tragic, 152
Forms, 4–9, 39–40. *See also* Culture; Life; Objectification

Goethe, Johannn Wolfgang von, 5, 128, 167; Simmel's book on, viii, 9, 36, 39n, 58; on women, 80, 116; erotic nature of, 108; on love, 173–77

Historical science: female contribution to, 77–81
Home: the housewife and, 23, 26–29, 70, 97–98; the nature of, 42, 90–94, 97

Ibsen, Henrik, 29n

Kant, Immanuel, 3, 5, 128; Simmel's book on, 4, 36, 39n, 56, 58; and the intellectualization of life, 36–38; and Simmel's rejection of reductionist thought, 38–39; categorical imperative of, 48; on sentience and understanding, 119; on art, 144; on egoism, 153; on morality, 170n, 182, 189